HOPE
*in the*
MAIL

## Also by Wendelin Van Draanen

*How I Survived Being a Girl*

*Flipped*

*Swear to Howdy*

*Runaway*

*Confessions of a Serial Kisser*

*The Running Dream*

*The Secret Life of Lincoln Jones*

*Wild Bird*

# HOPE
## in the
# MAIL

### Reflections on Writing and Life

## Wendelin Van Draanen

Alfred A. Knopf
New York

THIS IS A BORZOI BOOK PUBLISHED BY ALFRED A. KNOPF

Text copyright © 2020 by Wendelin Van Draanen Parsons
Jacket art used under license from Shutterstock

Visit us on the Web! GetUnderlined.com

Educators and librarians, for a variety of teaching tools,
visit us at RHTeachersLibrarians.com

Library of Congress Cataloging-in-Publication Data is available upon request.
ISBN 978-1-9848-9466-3 (trade) — ISBN 978-1-9848-9467-0 (lib. bdg.) —
ISBN 978-1-9848-9468-7 (ebook)

The text of this book is set in 11-point Scala Pro.
Interior design by Ken Crossland

Printed in the United States of America

January 2020
10 9 8 7 6 5 4 3 2 1

First Edition

Random House Children's Books supports the First Amendment
and celebrates the right to read.

# CONTENTS

# III·BEING A WRITER

# IV·SPECIAL CASES

# V·SEEDS AND SPROUTS

# VI·A PEEK BEHIND THE CURTAIN

# VII·FINAL THOUGHTS

# INTRODUCTION

Becoming a writer was nowhere near my top ten career choices. I wasn't one of those people who dreamed about penning the great American novel. Language arts was never my favorite subject in school. It bugged me, actually, because no matter how hard I worked at it, I couldn't seem to break the essay-writing code. My papers were invariably returned with little red marks all over them—edits, corrections, and questions that resulted in the dreaded "Redo" or, worse, B+.

The overachiever in me did not like the nebulous aspects of writing. The subjective assessment of it. She liked math. Where two plus two was always four, the square root of nine was always three, and the Pythagorean theorem was not built on shifting sands.

I was also not a journal keeper. I grew up with brothers and quickly learned that committing my thoughts and feelings and secrets to paper was a dangerous enterprise. Definitely not worth the risk.

And yet here I am, with over thirty books published and an unshakable belief that writing saved my life.

Or, at least, saved me from a life of bitterness and despair. When my path took some dark turns, it was writing that helped me sort out what I thought and felt and wanted. It helped me find empathy. It made me dig deep into the *why* of people's behaviors, and drove home the healing power of forgiveness. Writing gave me a new lease on life, and, perhaps most important, it helped me see past my own troubles to the needs of others.

Writing also taught me that everyone has a story. And it's our *collective* story—yours, mine, our neighbors' both close and far—that helps us navigate life. Our stories—our histories—can give new perspectives that assist us in seeing things more broadly or clearly. Hearing how others have endured or triumphed can give us the courage to slog forward through hard times or nagging doubts.

I've been speaking to audiences large and small, young and adult, for over twenty years now. Ostensibly I'm there to talk about my books or reading and writing, but my true mission is to inspire the audience to fight for their own dreams. When I'm addressing a gym full of students, I want them to come away feeling uplifted and ready to take on the world. Because the bottom line is, it's not *my* book or what *I've* gone through that matters most to them. What matters most to them is what *they're* going through. What *their* hopes and dreams are. Nothing adults say or preach or teach can hold a candle to what's going on in their lives right now.

It wasn't always, but speaking to a gym full of students is now easy for me. I make myself remember what it was like to be their age, to sit on a hard bench for an hour listening to an adult drone on about something that didn't matter to me. I promise myself never to be that adult, then try to present them with a talk that's lively and funny *and* substantive. It doesn't take long for the audience to figure out that I get them, and that I care. My favorite comments from kids include "I loved the parts where you were airborne!" (in reference to the way I leap around) and (the one I hear most often) "You should do stand-up!" But they've also taken away the core message: *Dream big, work hard, don't give up.*

Speaking to adults is not as easy for me. A sea of stony faces is much tougher to engage than bleachers full of squirmy kids. Confession: It took me quite a while to quit shaking in front of educators. After all, what authority did *I* have to speak to a banquet hall of language arts teachers and librarians when my background was in math and science? I hadn't read all the classics. I hadn't spent my life analyzing literature. Why was *I* at the podium? These were people who lived and breathed literature, people who bled red ink and had no problem spilling it all over my school assignments!

I felt like an impostor. But over time I came to realize that adults have many of the same longings and dreams for themselves that they had when they were sitting on a hard bench in a gym somewhere years ago—they've just learned to tuck them away behind the responsibilities of adulthood. A reminder that it's still okay to dream and to pursue our dreams is something we all need to hear. And when I was able to get past my own insecurities and actually *engage*, I found the audiences to be kind. Supportive. Encouraging. And (amazingly) they would come up to me afterward and suggest the stand-up thing too. Turns out, language arts teachers aren't a scary bunch after all. They're people with stories and pain and a need to laugh just like . . . well, everyone.

I've been asked by many people to collect the anecdotes and insights that I've shared with audiences during my twenty years of public speaking; to write them down.

So this is my story—not the boring autobiographical stuff, but the parts that pertain to writing and finding silver linings. The parts that I hope will make you want to follow whatever path you choose with guts and determination.

So come on. Let's get airborne.

· I ·

# YOUR VAULT

# 1

# WRITERS' GOLD

*Write what you know.* It's a good adage, and a manageable place to start. Many first novels are based on the author's experiences, so take a look at what treasures are already stored in your vault.

Before I was published (but after I had finally begun letting on to family that I was trying to be), an uncle of mine asked me how I thought I could possibly be a writer. "You're too young to be a writer. You need more experiences."

Gee, thanks. And yes, seeds of doubt can quickly grow into weeds in your garden of worthiness.

But here's the reality: No matter how young you are, you have experiences. You have *knowledge*. You have feelings and observations and thoughts that are worthy of exploration. You can arrive at conclusions that will broaden the thinking of others, or just paint a picture of life from your perspective. It's often the small stories with universal messages that touch us most deeply. We're all humans, trying to find a way forward, longing for the place where we feel at home.

My first published novel, *How I Survived Being a Girl*, was described as "*Seinfeld* for kids." What the reviewer meant was that it was a story about nothing, as the sitcom was famously called "a show about nothing."

Having your book be considered to be about nothing could be deflating, but I took it as a huge compliment. I loved *Seinfeld*. And saying that it was a show about nothing was as true as saying that it was a show about everything. *Seinfeld* was about both. It captured the human experience with humor and heart-zinging authenticity. It was a show about people living small lives in small apartments in a big city. No special effects, no outrageous sets. Just little glimpses into the lives of people muddling along.

All of us have that—a story about nothing that's actually about everything. No matter how ordinary your environment may seem to you, if your story can capture the human experience within it, others will relate.

Don't discount how extraordinary capturing the ordinary can be. And how difficult. You probably haven't viewed it this way, but if you're in school—as a student or as an educator—you are surrounded by writers' gold. How a school works, the voices of the kids and the administrators, the rules and limitations, the curriculum and expectations . . . it's all second nature to you. It's workaday stuff, part of the grind.

But let's turn that around. You have the background and details to write about a school environment naturally. The sights, the sounds, the smells, the mechanics of school life will flow from your fingertips. It's easy for you! Do you know how many authors—especially kid-lit authors—would *love* to know what you know? Maybe they were in school once, but that was probably a long time ago. Things in education have changed. To get it right, they have to work at it, and work hard.

Likewise, if you have a job—no matter how boring or ordinary you think it is—the way it works, the conversations in the employees' lunchroom, how your associates relate to each other and the *boss* . . . it's all gold.

If you're a dog walker, a babysitter, a dishwasher, a law clerk, a trash collector . . . it's all gold.

And if you're in a rough situation right now—turbulent home life, a bad neighborhood, even unemployed—turn it around. What you're going through is hard and dark and frightening, but it's also writers' gold. Take notes. Document your experience any way you can. There are seemingly mundane details about your everyday life that will give a natural authenticity to your writing.

It's all gold.

So pay new attention to the ordinary around you. Find the story inside it. And find the human connection, because the best stories are the ones that touch our hearts. Love, longing, triumph . . . these can be small and personal, yet they're universal desires. You don't have to save the world. Just save your character. And at the heart of that character is you.

So no matter what your situation is or how young you are, you have enough to paint a story with words, to make others hear you, see you, *feel* you.

Take a closer look at what you already know.

What's inside your heart?

What's inside your vault?

It's a really good place to start.

# 2

## OUT OF THE ASHES

What turns a person into a writer?

Sometimes the unexpected. I came to it from a place of anger and pain. Horrible stuff happened to my family when I was in college. An arsonist burned down our business—an industrial facility my immigrant parents had spent twenty years building—and then my father passed away unexpectedly six months later. We were devastated emotionally and financially, and our faith in justice was shaken to the core. I'd jolt awake in the middle of the night relieved to have escaped a nightmare, only to realize, *Oh, wait, no. That's my life.*

Unable to go back to sleep, I started writing. Scrawling, really, about how unfair the world was, how it was so wrong that such bad things could happen to good people, how small and helpless and lost I felt to be in the middle of this disaster, how the Big Bads—the people who had destroyed the business— were out there, free from any consequence of their actions.

I wouldn't classify what I did as journaling. It was more slashing at the paper. I was alternately furious and heartbroken, or maybe both at once. I felt raw and deeply wounded, and the facts, my thoughts, my emotions poured out, oozed out, bled out. I wrote and I wrote and I wrote.

And it didn't change a thing.

The Big Bads were still at large, no one came back to life, and there was still ash where dreams had once stood.

I started fantasizing about payback. Payback may be a bad idea, but the cornered, wounded animal doesn't care. The cornered animal is desperate and primed to strike back.

Fortunately, the weapon handy during my middle-of-the-night jolts into reality was a pen.

Fortunately, I discovered that I could kill off my bad guys on paper.

And unexpectedly, this led me to the world of fiction, where you don't have to stick to what really happened, where you can change the names of your bad guys a little, change the way things turn out a *lot*, and dole out payback that would land you behind bars if you tried it in real life. Torture, justice, murder . . . it was all available from the tip of a pen, no jail time required.

So, no. I didn't start writing with literary aspirations.

I started writing because I needed to kill off some bad guys.

Clearly, what I really needed was therapy.

Turns out, writing is *great* therapy.

# 3

## PUTTING HOPE IN THE MAIL

The first novel I wrote was an epic clash of good and evil. Weighing in at 627 pages, it had thinly concealed names, caricatured players, and a very visible ax to grind.

Yes, it was terrible.

But I didn't know that!

I also didn't know anything about publishing.

Well, other than that most publishing houses were located in New York City.

But now I needed to know! I had a masterpiece to place!

This was before you could query editors or agents or submit samples online. I got some preliminary information about the submission process by reading back issues of *Writer's Digest* magazine, then went to the library, checked out a book called *Literary Market Place*, perused it for friendly-sounding names, and started shopping my manuscript.

Compelling query letter—check!

Self-addressed stamped envelope—check!

Ignore the no-multiple-submissions rule because who has time for that?—check!

Not a great (or even good) strategy. And (displaying compounded ignorance here) I was also under the common misconception that getting a book published meant becoming an instant millionaire. Consequently, I thought that placing my manuscript would bring an end to my family's financial troubles. Or, at least, help out considerably.

So, yeah. Therapy and financial need. These were the forces fueling me. But then a strange thing happened. Each time someone in New York would agree to take a look at my full manuscript, I'd make a copy of it, box (yes, box) it up, and stand in line at the post office. And as I moved forward in the line, my heart would beat a little faster and I would tell myself that this was it. *This* editor was going to read and love my story. *This* editor was going to send me a million bucks and my family's financial troubles would be solved.

And when it was my turn at the counter, I'd give the box a quick kiss for luck, pay the postage, and walk away with a little spring in my step.

Outside, the world felt renewed with possibility.

Things were going to change!

We were *not* defeated.

Hope was in the mail.

# 4

## TODAY COULD BE THE DAY

I put hope in the mail for ten years.

Actively and persistently, I sent out manuscripts and queries, and for ten years I was actively and persistently rejected by editors and agents in New York.

The rejection slips were usually generic—some version of *We're sorry. This is not right for us at this time. But please think of us again with your next project.*

I shoved the slips inside a drawer.

Over time, they filled the drawer.

I moved them into a box.

Over time, they filled the box.

You'd think I'd have taken the hint: I didn't have what it took to be published. So why did I keep trying?

Looking back, I think it had a lot to do with keeping hope in the mail. As my first manuscript was making the rounds in New York, I began working on a second story. Another epic clash of good and evil! This time, though, it was more removed from my own story. Characters were becoming . . . their own entities. Plot was more . . . flexible. There was real freedom in that, and I enjoyed it.

I also began reading about the craft of writing. I read everything I could get my hands on because I wanted to finally crack the code. I wanted to get inside structure and dialogue, pacing and theme.

So when my self-addressed stamped envelopes started coming back to me with rejections for my first novel, I was disappointed, but not crushed. I'd learned more about craft and could see now that, yeah, the first book was more therapy than literature. I got back to work, thinking, *You didn't like that story? Okay, well, wait 'til you read this one!*

Having overlapping hope in the mail equipped me with the mantra *Today could be the day.* If I didn't give up, if I kept submitting, kept learning, kept writing, kept *trying,* someday someone somewhere would read one of my manuscripts and want to buy it.

*Today could be the day.*

It's a nice way to live your life, but it only works if you keep hope in the mail. This phrase doesn't refer to just physical mail or email. Putting hope in the mail means putting yourself—your work, your wishes—out there however you can. It means actively creating the *possibility* for good things to happen.

Now, prepare for your hopes to be dashed—because undoubtedly they will be. But when that happens, the only course of action is to pick yourself up, redouble your efforts, and put hope back in the mail. Don't let rejection or brusque (and occasionally cruel) critiques cause you to close in, close down, or give up. Don't sit in a dark corner licking your wounds. If you disagree with the opinions of the rejecting party, send your work to someone else. I promise you that over time rejection gets less painful and becomes just part of the process.

In the case of literature, it's *not* science, and I see now that that's a *good* thing. There is nothing more ho-hum than a formulaic book. And what one editor may dismiss, another editor *right next door* may love. So get back in the ring! And while you're waiting for a reply, shift your focus to a new project.

Do not wait around.

Nothing will reinvigorate you more than pouring your energies into something new.

Another thing that helped me endure ten years of rejection was not knowing it was going to be ten years. For all those years, I had a full-time job, and for many of them I also had two little kids. I got up each morning at five o'clock when my husband left for work, spent the next hour or so writing, then began my real day. I was constantly sleep-deprived. If I had known it would take ten years to get published, I almost certainly wouldn't have made it.

But I didn't know.

And every day I told myself, *Today could be the day.*

And then one day it was.

# 5

## DEFINING MOMENTS

Ten years is a lot of rejection for someone to take. And on the long and winding road to the day I finally got a "Yes," I heard things like "It's just too hard to get published" and "You have to know somebody in publishing" and "Maybe if you had an MFA, people would pay attention."

These, uh, *consoling* and, uh, *helpful* statements were tempting to buy into during the many phases of feeling discouraged. Maybe there were just too many obstacles, too many reasons I wouldn't succeed.

Any one of them would justify quitting.

So . . . what, then, made me keep going? Why did I think that, despite the odds, I could do this?

I trace the defining moment back to my first car.

A lot of kids I went to high school with got cars when they turned sixteen. Some got hand-me-downs, some got brand-new, off-the-car-lot, big-bowed beauties.

If I had asked my parents for a car of *any* kind, they would have laughed me out of the room. That's just not the way things worked in our family. If I wanted my own car, I was going to have to buy it with my own money.

Desperate for a vehicle, I scoured our small town for one I could afford. Taking out a loan or buying something on credit never even crossed my mind. We didn't do credit. We were taught to only buy what we could afford, and as a student without steady income, what I could afford would be paid for with money from babysitting, yard work, and summer jobs. This meant that what I could afford wasn't much, but there *were* three for-sale-by-owner prospects in town at my price point, and a friend offered to drive me around to check them out.

The first car was a classic Volkswagen Bug, which had a definite cool factor to it. The body looked straight—no big dings or dangling bumpers—but the interior was a different story. It wasn't just that the upholstery was thrashed, there was a big chunk of the floorboard missing. Like, you could see the *ground.* You could fit your *foot* through it!

When I asked the guy selling the Bug about it, he tried to convince me that it was cool. "It's like having a convertible," he gushed. "Only instead of seeing the sky go by, you get to see the road!"

Uh . . . no.

The second car was no better than the Bug. It looked like a demolition derby car, smashed flat enough that the doors didn't open. You got in by climbing through a window.

When we drove to the third location, I took one look at the

car and told my friend to just keep driving. It was a faded sky-blue Toyota Corona that had weird spots all over it. From our vantage point, it looked like it had been shot up by mobsters.

But as my friend was driving by at a crawl, she said, "Earl Scheib, ninety-nine ninety-five."

Earl Scheib had television commercials that ran in our region. His style was classic used-car salesman. He was enthused! The best! And he would paint your car for ninety-nine dollars and ninety-five cents.

I looked at my friend. "You think?"

She pulled over.

We got out.

We circled the car like it might be contagious and discovered that the spots that covered it weren't bullet holes. They were welts of rust.

But the interior was in good shape, the car ran great, and the guy came down fifty bucks.

I gave him my savings, named the car Bullet, and drove home feeling elated.

And then I learned that Earl Scheib wouldn't touch my car. "We don't deal with rust," they told me. "Even if we did, that thing's hopeless."

And now I felt trapped. I'd just spent my life savings on a car with incurable rust acne. There was no Clearasil for cars!

My dad, however, told me not to give up.

He had what he thought was a great idea.

"Why don't you just paint it yourself?"

Now, anyone who has done auto body work will know how absurd my dad's suggestion was.

I didn't.

The funny thing is, I didn't think I *couldn't* do it—I didn't *want* to do it. I knew it was going to be an enormous amount of work and that I'd never use any of the skills I picked up in the process. Like I was ever going to buy a car that needed painting again? I'd been an idiot to buy *this* thing.

So, no. I did not want to paint the car myself. And at first, I dug in. Resisted. But Dad wasn't offering to do it for me, and what choice did I have? Unless I wanted to abandon it or drive around in a car with ridiculous rust acne, I had to face this job.

I had to learn how to do it myself.

# 6

## PATCHING BULLET HOLES

For most of my life, my dad had owned his own business. It had started in our garage, had grown over time, and was now in an industrial part of town. It had heavy equipment and tools.

Lots of tools.

In addition to an air compressor (something he told me I'd need to spray the paint) and an assortment of sanding devices (with an even broader assortment of sandpaper), he brought home (deep announcer's voice, please) *the Milwaukee grinder.*

The Milwaukee grinder had already been through hell. It was dirty red, beat up, and heavy—I'm gonna say forty pounds. It *wasn't* forty pounds, but I'm gonna say it was anyway because that's what it felt like.

Dad had installed a wire brush on it, just for me. This nifty attachment was a metal cup with short, sturdy twists of steel protruding from the rim. Picture the Scrubbing Bubbles guy gone heavy metal.

Dad assured me that the Milwaukee grinder would make short work of the rust welts. He also made sure to tell me (and then remind me) that there should be *zero* rust left when I was done. If I didn't get rid of every last speck of rust, it would come back. Bubble up. Destroy the universe.

He ran an extension cord out to the street where my car was parked, gave me some safety tips (basically, don't kill myself), supplied me with a dust mask and safety glasses, plugged in the grinder, and let me pull the trigger.

The grinder shook me to the core. It felt like a wild animal, whining and growling, pulling hard on a chain. And when the whirring wire brush touched down on metal, it chewed it up and spit it out. Rust went flying everywhere!

I'm no wimp. I was pretty scrappy as a kid, and at this point in my life I had some heft to me. I'd recently beat my dad in a family arm-wrestling competition, so I guess he figured I could handle the grinder, because after he'd watched me blast a few welts to smithereens, he left me to obliterate rust on my own.

Many hours later, the asphalt around my car was a dusty orange, my body was jelly, and instead of rust welts all over it, poor Bullet was now full of holes.

"Hmm," Dad said, inspecting my giant auto sieve. "This will take a bit of Bondo."

Bondo.

Bondo is to car repair what Spackle is to wall repair. You know Spackle, right? That stuff you use to patch the hole a baseball or a broom handle or, say, a fist made in a wall?

You don't?

Well, if you live in a place with plasterboard walls, it's very handy stuff, meant for patching holes left by the removal of nails when repainting a room. You just apply a little to the hole, swipe across it with a putty knife (which is just a small metal spatula), let it dry, and repaint.

You can also use Spackle to repair larger holes (like from that baseball or broom handle or fist). But bigger holes require patience because Spackle will dry and shrink and crack, and if the hole is more than about half an inch in diameter, it will crater or collapse in the middle. With bigger holes you have to build up support on the edges, let the Spackle harden, and work your way in.

When you've finally patched a large hole and you think you've got it scraped smooth with the putty knife, you still have to take the time to sand it, because if you don't, what looks good as plaster will be revealed to be an ugly patch once it's painted.

I came to the Bullet repair with this handy bit of life experience already in my tool kit and set about patching the rust holes accordingly. I Bondo'd and I Bondo'd and I Bondo'd. For *days,* I Bondo'd. Then I sanded and I sanded and I sanded until I was just so sick of Bondo and sanding that I didn't *care* if the holes weren't perfect. They looked perfect enough to me.

There was never any doubt in my mind that I'd paint the car its original color—sky blue. I didn't want to mess with repainting the doorjambs or any of the interior detail, and a two-toned car (with clashing interior and exterior paint) is just wrong.

We lived in a somewhat rural community with limited options, and our town's car parts store didn't have much of a paint selection. When I told the clerk what I was looking for, he produced a can from a shelf by a large, sunny window and assured me a quart was all I needed. A smear of baby blue on the dusty lid served as the only color sample.

Back at car-painting headquarters on the street in front of our house, I covered the glass, chrome, and wheels of Bullet with masking tape and newspaper. Then my dad set me up with the air compressor, complete with long hoses, a canister, and a spray nozzle.

We transferred the paint into the canister, and that was the first time I laid eyes on the actual paint.

It was a bright robin's-egg blue, almost turquoise.

I hesitated but then told myself that the paint was just very concentrated and that, like paint in general, it would lighten as it dried. Plus, if a quart was plenty to paint the whole car, the color would thin out. It would be fine.

I shoved aside my concerns and focused on my dad's instructions. "It's all in the wrist," he told me, pantomiming the way I should wield the nozzle. "You want to go back and forth smoothly, in light layers. Don't build up too much or the paint will run."

I watched his demonstration, then tried it myself, imagining paint spraying from the nozzle. *Swoosh, swoosh.* I swayed a little, trying to get into the feel of smooth, fluid movement.

"I think you've got it," Dad assured me.

He turned on the compressor. I began swaying and pulled the trigger.

Out came bright turquoise paint.

I tried not to panic. I tried to be smooth. I tried to go in even, light layers. But I was distracted by the color. This was an *intense* turquoise, the kind you might see on a professional race car.

It didn't take long to realize that I didn't know what I was doing. And it was dawning on me that my dad didn't either. He'd sprayed paint on walls before, sure, but if you make a mistake on a wall, you can always follow up with a roller.

This was a completely different situation!

Then, as I moved around the car, trying to be smooth and go in even, light layers, the afternoon winds kicked up and created a rippling in the paint. Distracted by that, I stopped moving for a moment with the trigger pulled. Now there were drips! And as I hurried to get back into a smooth rhythm, I noticed that the holes I'd patched were showing themselves to be shallow craters.

This was a disaster!

By the time I was done, I was heartsick. All that work. All that time. All that money. And what did I have?

A turquoise turkey of a car.

# 7

## SHIFTING GEARS

For weeks I slumped way down in the driver's seat as I drove my turquoise turkey around, hoping nobody would recognize that it was me in that car. But what's funny is, I started having lapses in awareness. I started getting used to the way it looked. From inside it was easy to forget what it looked like on the outside as I focused on the task of driving. The radio blared happy sounds. And at Mach speed, who could possibly notice ripples and drips and craters? Bullet was just a bright turquoise blur.

Until the clutch went out.

It was a stick shift, of course. That's what my parents drove. It was the only practical choice, they claimed. How else would you push-start a car to life if the battery died?

I honestly cannot tell you how many times I helped push-start the family car. A jump start is fine, but it takes jumper cables and a willing second party who's game to squeeze their (typically more valuable) car into close proximity to yours and trust that you know what you're doing (since, usually, they don't).

No, it's much more practical to have your kids push from behind until you're rolling with enough momentum to pop the clutch and basically kick-start the motor.

Looking back, *practical* would have been for my parents to have a reliable car, but let's not go there.

The point is, I had no problem buying a stick shift because that was all I'd known growing up. But a stick shift meant Bullet had a manual clutch, and just as I was getting to a place of acceptance about the car's appearance, I began having problems shifting gears.

After a quick diagnosis, Dad determined that the culprit was my throw-out bearing—a little disc thingy at the heart of the clutch mechanism that disengages gears when the clutch pedal is depressed and reengages gears when the clutch pedal is released.

Lucky for me, Dad pointed out, there was a beat-up book in the bowels of Bullet's trunk that had the schematics for every part of my vehicle, with exploded diagrams and directions for how to change them.

Shaped like a thick metal bracelet, the throw-out bearing might have been a small (and relatively inexpensive) part, but getting to it turned out to be a task so big I wanted to cry. To replace it, I had to either pull the engine or drop the transmission.

My dad recommended I drop the transmission.

The operation took place on a Saturday in a corner of the

driveway of our home. Dad helped me jack up one side of the car so Bullet was on a slant, giving me enough space to work beneath it. Then he set me up with all manner of tools, wished me good luck, and left.

I lay under the car on the sandy cement, looking up at the belly of this beast. The whole undercarriage was coated in a hundred thousand miles of dirt-caked oil, a blackish-brown grime that was a quarter of an inch thick in some places.

Complaining about the ridiculous ick of the job wasn't going to get the part changed, so I took a deep breath and got to work. And the first step—draining the transmission fluid—turned out to be easy. I was intrigued by the thick liquid as it poured into the receiving pan, because it seemed incongruous to have a pinkish, sweet-smelling substance stored inside the ugly underbelly of this car.

But after that, things got messy. And hard. I scraped globs of gooey grime from all the bolts that held the transmission in place, both up by the clutch housing and back by the drive shaft. Then I figured out what size socket to use to loosen the bolts, attached the socket wrench to the first bolt, and pushed counterclockwise.

Nothing.

I got in better position and pushed harder.

Nothing.

I heave-ho'd, grunted and groaned.

Nothing.

I knew I was applying pressure in the correct direction because years before, my brother had taught me *Lefty loosey, righty tighty.* Still, the thing wouldn't budge. And after straining several more times to loosen the bolt, I decided that what I needed was more leverage.

I scooted out from under the car, rummaged through the garage, found a length of pipe, and stuck it on the end of the socket wrench.

Back under the car, I heave-ho'd again, both hands fisted around the pipe, pushing with all my might. This time the bolt gave way with a sudden *crack,* and in the process one fist slammed into the grimy undercarriage, busting open my knuckles.

Yes, pain. Yes, blood. Yes, swearing.

But I was also excited that the bolt was finally loose, so after blotting the blood and shaking off the pain, I focused on cracking the rest of the bolts, front and back. Then I lined up stacks of scrap two-by-four pieces beneath the transmission to keep it from crashing onto the driveway when the bolts came out.

One by one, I pulled out the bolts and clinked them into an old can for safe storage. And when they were all finally out . . .

Nothing happened.

The transmission just stayed up, in place, as if the bolts didn't matter.

I double-checked the schematic, reread the directions. I'd done everything the way I was supposed to, so why wasn't the tranny budging?

I shook it from the side.

Nothing.

I kicked it.

Nothing.

I knocked on it with a hammer against a block of wood.

Nothing.

I knocked harder.

Nothing.

Finally, I shoved aside the two-by-fours, got underneath the transmission, grabbed it with both hands, pushed with both feet, and . . .

Yeah . . . no.

Not yet.

First there was a sort of slurping sound. Then, as the front gasket broke its hundred-thousand-mile petrified seal, excess tranny fluid in the housing ran out and drenched me. Pink, sticky ick ran down my neck and into my ear and oiled back my hair.

And *then*, yes, *thunk*, the tranny came down.

Right on top of me.

Pinned to the driveway on my back with a transmission on my chest, I was scared and crushed and gasping for air, but mostly I was furious. Anger had been building inside me throughout the day, but this pushed me over the edge. Other dads bought their daughters new cars. Other dads would at least change the part for their daughter. But here I was under this turquoise turkey with a transmission on my chest! What kind of insane parents did I have?

But there's only so long you can stay pinned to the ground

31

by a transmission before you have to make a move. Spurred on by anger, I wrestled that metal monster off me, removed the throw-out bearing from the clutch housing, and marched into the house to confront my father, filthy face, busted knuckles, tranny hair and all.

I found him in his home office, paying bills.

"Here," I said, handing him the part.

He jumped from his chair. Now, I thought he might take one look at grimy, bloodied, beaten me and say something like *Oh, no! Are you all right?* But, instead, he jumped from his chair, his eyes fixed on the part, and said, "You did it!"

He grabbed his car keys and insisted we go right then to buy a new part. Daylight was burning! There was no time to lose! The next day was Sunday, and who knew what time the parts store would open, if they'd open at all!

He dropped me at the curb in front of Coast Clutch and Brake. I went inside, mortified. There were cute guys behind the parts counter. Cute guys who, when they saw me approach, elbowed each other like, *Oooh, baby,* and had a good chuckle over the Girl from Planet Grime.

I bought my part and got back in Dad's car, and I think he finally tuned in to how upset I was, because when we made it home, he helped me install the new part and bolt the transmission in place.

When we were done, I got in the driver's seat, fired up the motor, put the car in gear, let out the clutch, and . . . the car barely hobbled along.

It didn't work.

So, okay. *This* is when I broke down and cried.

But my dad said, "Don't give up now! It probably just needs to be adjusted."

As it turned out, he was right. A quick return trip to the underbelly for a simple adjustment was all it took. Afterward, I pulled out of the driveway tentatively, but half a block from home I was gunning it, changing gears, speeding up, downshifting through turns. . . . I didn't care what my car looked like. I didn't care what *I* looked like. I was consumed by a euphoria I hadn't experienced before.

I'd done it.

I'd fixed my own clutch!

Yeah, I'd been slimed and grimed and bloodied and crushed, but I'd come out victorious.

I'd done it!

It wasn't until people started asking me how I'd become tenacious enough to endure ten years of rejection that I began looking back on that day, that experience, with appreciation. Because despite how I felt about my father at that time, what I see now is that he gave me something much more valuable than a new car.

He gave me the belief that, with enough grit and determination, I could do anything.

· II ·

# WRITING

# 8

## FINDING YOUR VOICE

It might not have taken me so long to get published if I'd found my voice sooner. But I thought I had a voice, and I thought it was working just fine, thank you very much.

I didn't know that developing writers should be in search of their voice—the sound of combined words that feels right to them and rings true to the reader. As it turned out, my voice was located nowhere near where I was writing. I was looking—and writing—in all the wrong places.

When the events that spurred me toward writing occurred, I had just crossed into adulthood, so the voice I used to write about those events was that of an adult. And as time ticked along and my writing evolved beyond my own experiences and into those of actual fictional characters, I continued writing in the voice of an adult.

Turns out, my voice is not that of an adult.

Turns out, I'm stuck at about thirteen.

And despite all the angry therapy words I committed to paper, it turns out that my most natural voice isn't tragic or angry or injured—it's guardedly tender, but also funny.

My path to discovering this began when my husband gave me a copy of *Dandelion Wine* by Ray Bradbury. He said he loved it because he felt it captured the magic of growing up.

I loved it too. It reminded me of the mischief the neighborhood kids and I got into when we were growing up. It was a happier time in my life—time spent being outdoors, riding bikes, spying on the neighbors, and running a little wild. Reading *Dandelion Wine* made me mull over those years, and my new adult perspective could see the neighborhood and the people in it through a broader lens. There were layers to the adults I hadn't recognized as a kid. There were reasons, some dark and painful, that they behaved the way they did.

So I began writing what I thought of as my version of *Dandelion Wine,* and I did it in the voice of a twelve-year-old girl.

Early in the process something clicked, and clicked hard. I recognize now that it was the sound of me opening the vault and finding my voice. All of a sudden, writing was fast and fun and freeing. I laughed out loud, I teared up, I was *in the story.*

This was probably aided by the fact that I was working in a fictionalized version of a happier time of my life, but the fascinating thing about this is that, many years later, when hearing that the story was based on my childhood, my editor laughed and said, "I should have known," and told me that a lot of first books are based on the author's real life.

What all of this taught me about writing and about life is

that you should try to remain open to new paths. It's easy to become rutted in a certain way of thinking or an approach to life. We get comfortable with doing things a known way. It may not be the best way, but it's *our* way, and we tend to stick to it.

There may be discomfort in trying new ways, new things, but what's the harm, really? You can always go back to your old way.

So try a bite of something new. Try a different way home. Try a different kind of music, a different genre of fiction, a different color to wear. Just *try*. Give different a chance. You may discover whole new little worlds that suit you.

And you may just find your voice.

# 9

# FUNDAMENTALS

I'm not writing a mystery here. Or going for some great climactic moment. You already know I have published books, so clearly that story has a happy ending. And I *will* get to how that finally came together; however, in this section I want to focus on the mechanics of writing.

Please keep in mind that there is no right or wrong method. The things that work for me may not all work for you, but I still hope you'll find much that's useful in what I share. These are not writing *secrets,* they're things I've learned or discovered after years of working to crack the code—things that have helped me construct over thirty novels.

I'm happy to share them with you, but please assume that the phrase *In my view* precedes all the statements I make about writing, okay? I find qualifiers tedious both to write and to read, so let's just be done with the formality of that and get down to it.

There are three fundamental parts to consider when constructing a novel:

*Characters:* These are all the people who populate your story, not just the main character. You like them (or maybe hate them), they feel real, you care what happens to them, and you want to spend time with them.

*Story:* This is what happens, where it happens, and how you structure and pace it. The premise itself should be interesting, and the story should move along at a clip that will keep the reader's attention, with no sagging middle or unproductive sidetracks.

*Language:* This is the choice of words, their cadence, and the images they evoke. It can be anything from sublime prose to punchy, single-word sentences.

The good news is that if you can master two of the three, you will have a good book. The caveat is that one of the two must be compelling characters. You can paint glorious scenes with words or take us on a roller-coaster ride through the pages, but without compelling characters your story will have no heart.

So let's delve into each, but with the understanding that they cannot be fully isolated. *What* your characters do is the plot. *Why* they do it is based on who they are. And *how* their story or adventure is conveyed will include language that reflects who they are and what they are doing. It's all intertwined. Also, what further complicates an analysis by separation is that each of the threads is influenced by things that happen to the creator of the characters, their world, and their story. Because things that happen to the author in real life often influence what happens in the story or to the protagonist. And very often, it's this influence that gives the story heart.

So inseparable, yes, but I'll shift the focus to each and include some examples of life influences. Let's start with the one fundamental a good story cannot do without—characters with heart.

# 10

## THE CHARACTERS AROUND YOU

You absolutely, positively should not use cardboard when constructing your characters.

So, what should you use to create them?

You might want to start by going back to the vault and looking for inspiration there.

After years of searching for my voice in all the wrong places, I peeked inside my vault and discovered that back in a corner—behind what felt like a lifetime of other stuff—were the kids from my old neighborhood.

It had been ages since I'd seen them in person, but the memories surrounding them had been there all along, waiting. And when I took them out to play on the pages of my story, they surprised and delighted me by springing to life, becoming thinly veiled characters in a barely fictionalized world.

Fictional or not, the characters and their world were recognizable not only to me. When *How I Survived Being a Girl* was finally published, my mom urged me to get liability insurance. "What if the neighbors decide to sue you?" she asked.

*Sue* me? What was she talking about? We'd moved away ages ago. And who'd want to *sue* me?

But then I got to thinking about how the names of the characters in my book were barely different from the names of their real-life counterparts. Chuck was Charlie, Marilyn was Mary, Bill was Will, Andy was Little Andy. And the drunk next door was Freeko, which is what we'd called him in real life. There's even a map at the beginning of the book, pointing out where everyone lived, with FREEKO'S and an arrow pointing to the house next door.

Keeping everything so close to the way it had been did translate to a sense of reality on the page, but I hadn't exactly stretched my creative abilities, and my mom had a point.

Deniability on my part would be difficult.

Still, I tried to put my mom's worries to rest. "Come on, Mom," I scoffed. "Who in their right mind would stand up in a court of law and say, 'I am Freeko and I take issue with the way I'm portrayed in this book'?" But for the first time I became concerned about other people's reactions to characters I created. I'd been *not* published for so many years that having a book out there for anyone to read had just been theoretical to me.

But now it was real.

Had I made a huge mistake?

After mulling it over for a while, I dialed the old number for "headquarters"—the house that shared a back fence with ours when I was growing up. It was the house where the neighborhood kids knew to congregate, the house where the Myers family lived.

The Myers family, who became the Moyers family in the book.

Cringe.

Anyway, I wasn't sure the number would still be in service, but Mr. Myers answered on the third ring. When I said who I was, he said, "Well, now. This is certainly a voice from the past."

After some pleasantries, I got to the point, explaining that I'd written a book about growing up in the neighborhood and that I hoped when they read it they'd take it in the spirit intended. I might have mentioned that they were the Moyers in the book and about Marilyn being Mary and Chuck being Charlie and Bill being Will.

I hadn't bothered to change their dog's name, so I didn't mention that.

Mr. Myers seemed more interested in how everyone in my family was doing, so the conversation veered off in that direction and then we were saying our goodbyes.

Before I'd managed to fully exhale my sigh of relief, the phone rang.

It was *Mrs.* Myers.

"What's this about a book?"

I explained all over again, and again I said that I hoped they'd take it in the spirit intended.

Fortunately, they did. They actually thought it was a lot of fun to have that time captured as fiction, with enough true events woven in to create a little capsule of our childhood.

And Freeko? He and his wife were no longer living there. I don't know what happened to them and I didn't dig too hard to find out. I now recognize the difficult nature of their situation, but as a child I did not. And thirty books later, I regret not exploring key threads—like the Freekos—with more depth. At the time I was unable (or, perhaps, unwilling) to venture far from the events and characters of my real childhood, but now I see the missed opportunity inside the story, the deeper paths that were waiting right there for me to explore.

It didn't take thirty books for me to learn this valuable lesson—I caught on after the first one: Good fiction can be seeded in reality but should be given the chance to grow beyond it. New writers especially find it hard to deviate from events as they actually happened, but learning to let go of reality is key. When we're too tied to how things really were, our imagination is shackled.

So pulling characters directly from my vault was a shortcut. What I would recommend instead is that you springboard from what's stored away inside yours and let your characters evolve into their own entities—something I will delve into more later. Because if you find that your story is following the plot and people of real-life events so closely it might be considered nonfiction, or if someone says, *Hmm, you might want to get liability insurance,* you probably should take a step back.

Give your characters some room to grow.

Let your story breathe on its own.

True creative freedom begins with letting go.

# 11

# GROWING PAINS

After I'd discovered that I loved writing in the voice of a kid, the next character I began developing was a teen sleuth I named Samantha (Sammy) Keyes.

This time, I had no specific person in mind when I envisioned the character. Sammy was a hybrid of my past and my present. At this point I was a high school teacher, and Sammy became a sort of amalgamation of people and traits and was definitely influenced by the students in my classroom. Skateboard, high-tops, jeans, a quick wit, and attitude . . . that's where I began.

And what kind of kid was she?

Poor. I knew that much. I also knew she lived in a bad part of town in a seniors-only highrise with her grandmother. I knew that she felt abandoned by her mother, that her father was a mystery, and that she felt trapped by her difficult circumstances.

At the beginning of writing a book, you may think you know your main character, but the key to creating without cardboard is to acknowledge that—as with people in real life—it will take time and *effort* to really get to know them.

So this time, instead of moving old friends around the page, I opened my heart up to a new one and allowed her to grow on me.

I liked Sammy from the get-go. And spending time with her—getting to know her—was something I looked forward to each day. I found myself thinking about her and her story all the time. So much so that as *Sammy Keyes and the Hotel Thief* wrapped up, I wasn't ready to say goodbye.

She'd become a friend I wanted to spend more time with.

But as with any new friendship, you can't be sure how long it will last. At the time, I had no way of knowing that Sammy and I would evolve together through eighteen books. At the time, all I knew was that there were big things in her life that weren't settled. Sure, she'd solved the mystery and gotten back at her archenemy—the sneaky and vindictive Heather Acosta—which was all very satisfying. But she was still living illegally with her grandmother, her mother was still MIA, and she still didn't know who her father was.

So I kept thinking about her.

And she kept growing on me.

And so I began working on *Sammy Keyes and the Skeleton Man,* a story that sprang from something kids in my classroom were whispering about—the same thing kids whispered about every year as Halloween approached: doing a ding-dong-ditch at the Bush House.

The Bush House was considered the spookiest house in town, which was actually kinda pathetic. There was no peaky-pointy roof, no creaky sounds or slamming shutters, no bats in the belfry. It didn't even have a belfry. It was a little box of a house much like the one my husband and I were renting, only completely obscured by bushes.

Ooooh. Spooky.

The Bush House was located only a couple of blocks down the street from us, and I ran by it all the time, sometimes with a child in the baby jogger and our two big Siberian huskies in tow, sometimes by myself. You really couldn't see the house for the bushes, which started at the sidewalk and grew taller toward the structure, but still. Why was the ring-and-run thing *such* a thing?

Having overheard my students plotting, I decided to try to put a stop to their plans. "Please," I said, "just leave that poor man alone." I told them how I'd heard he'd become reclusive after his wife had died and that he'd just given up on things.

But one of the students said, "Oh, Ms. Van Draanen, haven't you heard? He *murdered* his wife!"

"Yeah," another chimed in. "He murdered his wife, and he lives in that house eating rats!"

"Rats? And *murder*?" I squealed. "Who believes that?"

Well, *they* did.

During school, I was not connecting this in any way to

Sammy Keyes. And that night, when I was out on my own for a little sanity jog and came upon the Bush House, I was still thinking only of the kids in my classroom. And, a little stewed about their ridiculous need to ding-dong-ditch a poor, depressed man, I made an impulsive move.

I cut up the walkway to go meet the Bush Man myself.

My plan was to explain that the kids in my classroom harassed him because they thought he was a rat-eating monster who'd murdered his wife, and ask him what had really happened so I could relay it to them and maybe put a stop to the stupid ding-dong-ditch thing.

I was still not thinking about Sammy Keyes. I was simply preoccupied with how to word things politely.

And then suddenly, I found myself in darkness.

The bushes had become thick and tangled, connecting overhead to create a craggy tunnel. It was like someone had clicked off the streetlights, and there was no light coming from the house. The temperature also seemed to have dropped. A lot! What had seemed like out-of-control-but-not-at-all-scary bushes from the sidewalk were now thick, thorny claws reaching out to grab me.

My mind went into panic mode. These were no longer bushes, they were BOOOOSHES! And I started thinking there might be an ax murderer in these BOOOOSHES who was going to hack me into little bits and hide me in the BOOOOSHES and I'd never see my babies, ever again!

So, yeah. I chickened out.

But as I was thinking about the incident later, picturing

my students getting up to the door, *that's* when Sammy Keyes appeared in my mind. That's when my writer's imagination kicked in. I could just see Sammy and her friends making it all the way up to the Bush House door, but when they get there, whoa! There's no electricity. How can you ding-dong-ditch when the doorbell doesn't work? But they sure don't want to have made it so far and fail. So, *bam, bam, bam,* they pound on the door.

Only the door's not latched, and it *creeeeeaks* open.

And inside they see . . .

Well, you get the idea. I took the teens, the house, the fear, the mischief, reworked them and infused them into a story. And as it unfolded, I discovered things about Sammy—the depth of her kind heart, the way she can muster strength and bravery when faced with danger . . . or mean kids at school. And as I spent more time with her, she became more and more real to me.

At this point in my life I had a one-year-old and a three-year-old and I was working full-time. I had a standard school schedule; my husband had Tuesdays and Wednesdays off and worked weekends. It was a constant juggle, and the only time we weren't working, writing, or parenting was Thursday nights, when we had a standing date to watch *Seinfeld.*

Sammy was on my mind first thing in the morning, when I'd steal some time to write before the kids woke up, and at night after the kids were in bed. I thought about her when I was driving, jogging, vacuuming. . . . I did chores puzzling out plot and imagining scenes in my mind.

With each day she was becoming more and more real to me.

And then one morning, about halfway through the writing of *Skeleton Man,* I woke up with a little bit of a song playing through my head. The melody was kind of bluesy and went, *Sammy Keyes and the Sisters of Mercy* . . . Through the darkness, I actually said, "Who are the Sisters of Mercy, and what are they doing singing in my head?"

Sammy Keyes had fully invaded. I saw her, heard her, *felt* her everywhere, and now she'd moved into my dreams, presenting me with new characters in her world.

Who were these *Sisters?*

As I moved forward in my day, they followed me, growing brasher and wilder in my imagination. By the end of the day, I knew they weren't your average nuns in habits or sensible gray skirts. These were *wild* nuns. Ones who wore purple feather boas and purple spandex pants and put on rock 'n' roll shows to raise money for the homeless.

And with these new characters, a whole new story idea for Sammy was shaping up in my mind.

The evolution of this is valuable in that it illustrates how fictional characters can invade an author's world and create a sort of alternate universe, one that houses characters who feel so real to the writer that they come across as real to the reader.

So let your characters in. Make the effort to spend quality— and quantity—time with them. Let them dance around your mind. Let them occupy your heart.

Only then will they come alive on the page.

# 12

## KNOCK-KNOCK

It's not just that the more time you spend with characters, the better you know them and the more real they seem; it's also that they take on a life of their own.

Which is always weird.

Weirder still is the realization that your characters have begun influencing *you*.

How can that be, when we're the ones controlling them? It becomes a huge mental Möbius strip. And although the goal is to make yourself invisible in the story so your reader forgets who's moving the plot and people along, it's truly strange when your character turns things around on *you*.

The first time this happened to me was while I was writing *Sammy Keyes and the Sisters of Mercy*. It was the weekend, a late fall evening. My husband was at work. The huskies were in the backyard. I was home with our kids (who were now two and four years old), catching up on housework.

I remember being up to my elbows in suds, doing the dishes and running through some plot scenarios for *Sisters of Mercy* in my mind. So far in the story, Sammy had discovered that there was a girl about her age living alone in a camouflaged cardboard box on the outskirts of town. At the moment, Sammy was trying to figure out some way to help her. She didn't want to risk going to the police—her relationship with the grumpy and suspicious Officer Borsch was already hazardous to her own living situation. Plus, the homeless girl was furious with Sammy for following her, and adamant that she not tell anyone about her. A runaway from bad foster care, she was terrified of being placed back in the system. And Sammy couldn't exactly invite the girl to stay at the Senior Highrise with her—she wasn't supposed to be living there herself!

Still, Sammy was determined to help her. Rain was in the forecast. She *had* to figure out something.

So, there I was, at the sink, deep into visualizing the next scene, when someone knocked on the front door.

The kids zipped over and looked out the window. "It's a lady!" my four-year-old announced.

I dried my hands and opened the door, and through the heavy security screen I saw a woman about my age wearing a loud pink dress and dirty sneakers. Her face was deeply tanned and weathered, and she was carrying a bulging pillowcase.

I'd had enough homeless people on my porch to recognize the signs. And I guess she'd had enough doors closed in her face to recognize *those* signs.

"Wait!" she said, reading my mood. "I was just hoping you would dry my clothes. They're washed, I promise!" She looked out at the cloudy sky. "There's just not enough daylight left to dry them outside, and I really want to get out of this dress."

I had a kid wrapped around each leg, peering at her from behind me. I had my own laundry to do and dry. And who knew if there were lice in her clothes? Could lice survive the wash? Wait. There was no Laundromat nearby, so how had her clothes even been washed?

My experience with the homeless was uneven. Who knew *anything* about this situation? Maybe this was a trick? I had my kids to protect!

And that's when a little voice in my head said, *Sammy wouldn't close the door. Sammy would help her.*

And *that* was the moment my character started moving *me* around.

"Go to your room," I commanded my kids, and when they scurried off, I went outside to better assess the situation.

She hefted the pillowcase. "They're clean, I swear."

I pointed to the bench on our porch. "Sit right there."

When I took her pillowcase, she let out a huge breath. "Oh, thank you!"

I went inside. I closed and locked both doors. I loaded her clothes in our dryer and put the heat on high. Then I got back to the dishes.

Which felt absurd.

This poor woman, out at dusk in the gathering cold in a

55

bright pink dress, looking for a way to dry her clothes. I wasn't ready to invite her in, but I could at least go *out*, maybe offer her something to eat?

First I let the dogs inside. Then I checked on the kids. Then I went outside, leaving the front door open and the security screen closed.

"Beautiful dogs," she said as I sat down on the porch step. "Your kids, too." And before I could reply, she said, "I have two boys about their ages. They took them from me, but . . ." She fought against tears, and I did too. And for the next forty-five minutes I hung out on the porch with her. The kids eventually came out, as did the dogs.

There *was* food involved, but it wasn't a party or anything. The whole time, there was an obvious wariness on both our parts. She let on that she spent nights with a few other people behind some bushes near the mall, but the walls went up when I asked her about social services. She was not interested in discussing it or having me try to connect her with help. She just wanted her clothes.

When they were dry and back in her pillowcase, I handed them over and asked, "Do you have a jacket somewhere?" because there wasn't one in the clothes I'd dried.

"I'll be all right," she said. "I just layer up."

I couldn't imagine nights in the bushes without a jacket, so I made her wait while I decided which one of the three I owned I wanted to give her. She was completely jazzed to get my teal Lands' End, and she put it on right away.

Then she left, teal jacket over bright pink dress, stuffed pillowcase in hand.

Already in *Sammy Keyes and the Sisters of Mercy*, Sammy had had a revelation about her living situation. Up until she'd discovered the homeless girl living in the cardboard box, she had grumbled about how bad things were for *her*—how she had to sleep on her grandmother's couch and sneak in and out of the building, how everything she owned had to fit in her grandmother's bottom dresser drawer. . . . She was definitely disgruntled.

But on the walk home from following the girl to her cardboard box, Sammy starts to see her own situation in a new way: Maybe she has to sneak home via a fire escape, but at least she has a roof over her head. At least she has a couch to sleep on. At least she has a grandmother who looks out for her and loves her.

And in a parallel-universe twist of the Möbius strip, as the homeless woman walked away, I saw my own situation in a new way: Maybe it was intermittently leaky, but at least I had a roof over my head. At least I had a jacket to wear, food to eat, and kids I could care for and hug.

So maybe, like Sammy, I needed to focus on what I had, instead of what I was lacking.

As future stories unfolded, I learned to listen to my characters more closely. I let them teach me to be braver, kinder, more patient, more reflective, even funny. As writers, we create characters, but they, in turn, can mold us into better versions of ourselves if we let them. It's strange and surreal . . . and also truly awesome.

As to the homeless woman in pink, I never saw her again.

And I'm sure she has no idea that *Sammy Keyes and the Sisters of Mercy* is dedicated to her.

# 13

# BACKSTORY

I had completed three Sammy Keyes mysteries and still didn't have an offer on any of them.

So I started on the fourth.

Logical, right?

Yeah . . . no. But here's the thing: I felt I had to write it because Sammy *did* feel like a real person to me now. And although the mystery was resolved at the end of *Sisters of Mercy,* big things in Sammy's life were still up in the air. And, most unsettling of all for me, she was carrying around a lot of not-so-buried anger. Even if the books would never be published, I couldn't leave Sammy like that. For her to be okay, I knew she had to have a revelation about forgiveness that would help her deal with her anger.

For her own sake, she had to find a way to forgive her mother for leaving her.

So I started writing *Sammy Keyes and the Runaway Elf,* with the heart of both the story and the mystery centering around forgiveness.

Back on the first page of chapter one of *Sammy Keyes and the Hotel Thief,* Sammy tells us that whenever she asks her grandmother why their nosy neighbor Mrs. Graybill is such a bitter old woman, her grandmother shrugs and says, "It happens to people sometimes," and then changes the subject.

Maybe Grams says that because she really doesn't know much about Mrs. Graybill. Or maybe *I* was the one who really didn't know enough about Mrs. Graybill, so how could Grams?

*Sammy Keyes and the Runaway Elf* became a book of reckoning. Not for my characters, but for me. This is the book where I realized that a character's backstory—their fairly detailed history—mattered. Even if it never made it onto the page, I needed to know each character's history and their secrets. To truly understand the person they were, for their actions and evolution to make sense, I had to analyze their past.

Also, in the first chapter of the first book a question had been posed about a character's backstory that, three books later, still hadn't been answered. That's like introducing a weapon in your story and never using it. Why'd you put it in there? Good writing requires that you either remove it or use it.

I went with use it—it was time to answer Sammy's question. Why *was* Mrs. Graybill such a crabby old bat?

What began as the exploration of one character's backstory blossomed into establishing histories for all my main characters. I spent hours and hours imagining their pasts, and feeling their dilemmas and joys and pain. I figured out who Sammy's father was. No, I didn't know who he was when I began, and when I figured it out, I was able to understand Sammy's mother much better. I also got beneath Officer Borsch's thick crust, saw Grams's past unfold, and spent some serious time inside Heather Acosta's troubled mind.

In the process of doing this for my characters, I found myself doing the same sort of analysis of the people in my real life.

It was strange. And enlightening. Looking in real depth for possible reasons behind people's behaviors was new to me, and doing so created an astonishing shift inside me. Where I used to be sucked into arguments or get my buttons pushed, I could now step back and look at those situations with a sense of curiosity. And instead of using the weapons I kept at the ready for the people who seemed to like to antagonize or criticize, instead of hitting back with justifications or counterattacks, I put those weapons down.

I pushed them aside.

And my new mantra became *I will not take the bait. I will not fight with you.*

Once again, writing was teaching me how to be a more compassionate person. We all have people who stress us out or push our buttons or are just unpleasant to be around. The easiest thing may be to avoid those people, but sometimes that's not possible. Or, in order to see some people, we have to put up with others (the classic Thanksgiving scenario). In those cases I've found that figuring out *why* people behave the way they do really reduces the tension or the sting or just the *annoyance* of having to deal with them. Chances are good that they won't change, but your reaction to them will, and that's a crucial improvement.

So now, if I can get to the *why* of a person's behavior—which I've found is usually rooted in feelings of insecurity or inadequacy—I can usually substitute my flash emotions (anger, irritation) with understanding, and even sympathy. When you understand what's driving the abrasive behaviors, you can get to a place where your irritation doesn't flare. It's a much more pleasant state of being.

The bonus of this new approach to antagonistic or annoying people is that in cases where you just *can't* conjure up sympathy—for those dyed-in-the-wool jerks—you can learn a lot from their example about how *not* to be.

No one wants to evolve into being a Mrs. Graybill. No ten-year-old kid says, *When I grow up, I want to be a crabby old bat.* So why are there so many crabby old bats out there? Usually, it's not one big thing that shapes a person's attitude, it's a collection. Things happen in degrees. Disappointments accumulate. Attitudes shift. Grudges collect. And the youthful exuberance of *Anything's possible* can devolve into the jaded view that life's not fair and then you die.

Don't become that person.

And if you find yourself around people who are like that, don't let them blindfold you with their negative attitude and lead you down their dark dead end. Because, although they will never in a million years admit this, they welcome your defeat because it makes them feel better about their own.

Misery does indeed love company.

I would never have guessed that spending time with fictional characters could impact my real life so much. That the process would teach me that no matter how old you are, you should fight against losing your youthful exuberance with everything you've got. That you should instead find sympathy for the people who have replaced their dreams with bitterness, and firmly resolve not to become like them.

But that's the magic of writing.

Of getting to know your characters.

They can guide you to your own awakenings.

# 14

## TREES AND ROCKS

Shifting the focus for a moment to story structure, with an eye here on plot.

Plot is simply what happens with and to your characters, and I've found there's much value in the common plotting advice to put your protagonist up a tree . . . and then throw rocks at them.

If you want to bore your reader out of their mind, write about someone who is perfect or whose life is perfect. There's no payoff, no tension, when things run too smoothly. It's the struggle, the *want*, that gets us rooting for the protagonist.

So, if you create a main character (the protagonist) that readers like and make their life hard, either physically or emotionally (put them up a tree), and have them overcome a lot of obstacles (dodge a lot of rocks) in order to end up in a better place, your readers will root for them to succeed. They will *care*. They will *want* to read—and keep reading—your story.

So, okay. Writing 101. Find a tree. Load up with rocks and then . . .

Let those rocks fly.

At first you won't want to. At first you'll have the urge to protect your protagonist.

Get over it.

Do your story a favor.

Throw the rocks.

The tree I put Sammy Keyes in is the seniors-only apartment building. She's not supposed to live there, so she has to use the fire escape to sneak in and out of the building. This provides a whole arsenal of rocks. There's so much potential for things to go wrong.

Other rocks include nosy neighbor Mrs. Graybill, who suspects Sammy is living there and is determined to prove it (and if she does, Sammy and her grandmother will be evicted). Also, Sammy doesn't know who her father is, and Lana Keyes—Sammy's diva mother, who has left her behind to pursue an acting career—won't tell her.

Rocks, rocks, and more rocks.

And the biggest rock of all?

At the beginning of *Hotel Thief*, Sammy is entering the seventh grade (which, in my experience, was an *avalanche* of rocks), and she starts the school year off by clashing with mean girl Heather Acosta.

After years of attending the School of Hard Knocks of Writing, I had my battle plan mapped out when I began writing *Sammy Keyes and the Hotel Thief*. I was locked and loaded, ready to let some rocks fly!

The first chapter—about ten pages—pounded out pretty effortlessly.

I did not start with long passages about Sammy's situation. I started with action.

In the opening pages, Sammy is looking out of her grandmother's bedroom window with binoculars, giving us the lay of the land. She tells us about things she's seen in the neighborhood and how the binoculars have saved her from feeling trapped in an old, decrepit building with old, decrepit people. And after we're introduced to a few landmarks, she tells us about the Heavenly Hotel—the big, pink, seedy flophouse across Broadway—which is the one place her grandmother has forbidden her to look at with binoculars.

And yet she accidentally *does* look, and she happens to see a suspicious-looking man in the window of one of the Heavenly's rooms. He's wearing black gloves and he's pawing through a woman's purse.

She quickly concludes that this is a burglary in progress. Now, under normal circumstances she would probably call 911, but these aren't normal circumstances. And 911 operators want to know things like who you are and where you live and what you're doing looking into hotel windows with binoculars.

For Sammy, that's a huge can of worms, much too dangerous to open.

She also can't tell her grandmother. Grams would be furious that she'd been spying on people in the hotel. Even though Sammy wasn't *spying* spying, she'll never be able to explain it.

So there she is, way up a tree, way out on a limb.

Does she put the binoculars down?

Duck and hide?

No! We've just begun. We can't let her out of the tree yet!

Instead, Sammy leans in.

She gets the focus tight on the binoculars.

And just as she realizes she's seen the thief before . . . that she knows him from somewhere, but where? . . . he looks up and sees her looking at him.

Gasp!

I ended the chapter there.

Cliff-hanger!

Oh, yeah!

It felt like I was onto something really special, so I printed the pages and held my breath as my husband read them. I tried to act all nonchalant and occupied with other things as I secretly watched him. I wanted to see him react, wanted to hear that he felt like I did about the beginnings of this story.

He smiled at me when he was done and said, "It's really good."

I was immediately crushed. Everyone knows *good* is not good. *Good* is "interesting." *Good* is awful.

"No, really!" he said. "It's great!"

I studied him. He was obviously holding back. "But . . . ?"

He hesitated, then confessed. "I thought she was going to wave at the guy."

My breath caught.

*Wave* at the guy?

She had mentioned waving at people down on the street, but . . . at the thief?

That would be an insanely stupid thing for her to do! The thief would know beyond a shadow of a doubt that she had seen him, that she had been *studying* him. And he would know exactly where Sammy lived. Waving would be disastrous!

Which meant that it was a *brilliant* idea.

I added the wave, and it became a defining moment in the creation of Sammy Keyes. That simple action says so much about who she is. Instead of my describing with words that she's impulsive and fearless and a bit of a loose cannon, a single action painted that picture.

That scene is a great example of how you should *keep throwing rocks* at your protagonist when they're up a tree—even when it makes you cringe.

That wave was definitely a rock.

A big, crazy rock.

One that Sammy threw, right at herself.

Also, the easiest way for us to get to know people in real life is to see how they react in stressful situations. There is no better way to expose a person's true colors. So use rock-throwing in your writing and let it serve a dual purpose. When you're crafting your story, create situations where the *actions* of your characters further define who they are while simultaneously moving the plot forward. When Sammy waves, it conveys volumes about her, but it also makes us want to keep reading.

I mean, what's the thief going to do now that he's seen her? Sammy's impulsiveness has gotten her into big trouble. Turning the page is the only way to find out just how big, and how she's going to get out of it.

# 15

## VILLAINS

One of the main "rocks" you will throw at your protagonist is an antagonist, who can be anything from a somewhat thorny competitor to a full-blown villain.

I do so enjoy playing with a full-blown villain—something I embraced early on.

In addition to the therapeutic need to kill off (on paper) some of the family disaster Big Bads, I also discovered the (admittedly childish) joy of getting back at a certain Little Bad from my childhood inside the pages of *Sammy Keyes and the Hotel Thief.*

The avalanche of rocks that was my middle school experience was shaken loose by a girl who saw me as an easy target. Since I had frugal parents, my back-to-school wardrobe consisted almost entirely of hand-me-downs from a neighbor girl who was three years older than I was. Every year, her mom took her shopping, and, from underwear to dresses, the girl cleared space for her new wardrobe by bagging what she no longer wanted and delivering it to me.

Because I was younger and quite scrawny, none of her clothes ever fit me, but I actually loved getting the hand-me-downs. It was better than shopping with Mom, who was impatient with the process and convinced that two outfits and a pair of shoes should be adequate for a school year. I really, really wished our public school had had uniforms. Maybe Little Bad wouldn't have noticed me so quickly. Maybe I would have found it easier to fit in.

Looking back, I see that Little Bad was just your garden-variety bully. She had stringy blond hair and piggy eyes, but somehow she made me feel like the ugly one. She made fun of the way I dressed, the way I walked, that fact that I brown-bagged it instead of eating cafeteria food, the fact that I'd raise my hand in class with answers . . . you name it, she found ways to ridicule me.

And yeah, maybe my tailoring skills weren't the best when it came to taking in the hand-me-downs, maybe the elastic in the undies was shot and I had to slyly hitch them up every few steps, maybe I was a little too exuberant with my hand-raising in class, but wow, the names.

And she didn't stop at name-calling. She and her friend would follow me into the girls' bathroom, enter the stall next to mine, hop onto the toilet rim, look over the divider, and heckle me as I tried to relieve myself.

And then there was the harassing me for money. She knew I didn't carry any, yet every day she'd make a point to ask, then tease me for being "worthless."

One day Little Bad came up to me at the lunch tables, where I was already deep into my brown bag. She had a sneer on her face, which wasn't unusual, but this time something was different, though I couldn't put my finger on what.

"Give me your money," she demanded.

I sighed and shook my head. "You know I don't have any money."

What was different turned out to be that Little Bad was packin' steel. She had a sewing pin on her, and in a flash, she'd drawn it like a mini-sword and was jabbing me in my derriere.

Okay. It wasn't a sword. Or even a knife. It was just a sewing pin.

But it really, really, *really* hurt.

And compounding the pain was the shock of it. I mean, why? What had I done? Why was she so *mean* to me?

Little Bad sneered, flicked the pin on the ground, and hurried off laughing.

And me? I never forgot the way that felt.

Fast-forward to the writing of *Sammy Keyes and the Hotel Thief.* I could have placed Sammy in elementary school . . . but there weren't enough rocks in my elementary school experience. Or I could have put her in high school, but again, not enough rocks. Angst, sure, but by then we'd moved to a new town, I'd joined the track team and had some good friends. I was doing okay.

So, with the tree-and-rocks thing firmly in mind, and knowing the story would seem more real if I could feel the pain of zinging rocks myself, I stuck poor Sammy in the seventh grade and I gave her someone like Little Bad—I gave her Heather Acosta.

Much of the way Heather acts in *Hotel Thief* is styled after the way Little Bad treated me. She makes fun of Sammy's clothes and calls her a loser. She also asks her for money, and when Sammy tells her she doesn't have any, Heather jabs her in the rear end with a sewing pin.

Up to that moment in the writing of the story, I was in control of my character. But after that jab, everything changed. Sammy stopped being an extension of my experiences and became herself. Because Sammy didn't just sit there, taking the abuse. *Uh-uh-uh.* She got off the lunch bench, followed Heather through the tables, turned her by the shoulder, and then, *bam,* punched her in the nose. Blood went squirting everywhere!

It was five in the morning when I was writing this scene. It was still dark outside. I was sitting at the little desk in our bedroom, typing at the keyboard, watching the words spill from my fingertips as Sammy went absolutely *rogue.* My heart began pounding, *ka-blam, ka-blam,* my fingers were shaking, and I was suddenly popping with sweat.

Then the punch happened, and before I knew what I was doing, I leapt onto the bed and jumped up and down like a madwoman, crying, "Yeah! Yeah! Oh, yeah!"

It took a little while, but when I started coming down from

the euphoria of bloodying the nose of the fictionalized version of my archenemy from seventh grade, I realized, Oh.

Oh, *maaaaaan*.

Here I was, a mother. A *teacher*. What kind of example was I setting? I know you're not supposed to go around punching people out! You're supposed to resolve your differences in a civilized manner.

And since there are—or should be—consequences to your actions, I wound up suspending Sammy Keyes from school her first day of seventh grade.

Clearly, Sammy is a flawed character. But after she threw that punch, I couldn't wait to spend more time with her. With that punch she'd become my new best friend. Or, at least, the friend I wished I'd had in middle school. The one who'd have stuck up for me around Little Bad. The one whose heart's in the right place, even if her fist sometimes winds up in the wrong place.

As the story unfolded and the page count mounted, Heather Acosta morphed away from being a fictionalized Little Bad. Little Bad could only dream of being as smart or as devious as Heather Acosta would become. But Little Bad was a good place to start. Good clay to mold.

The sweet revenge in this is not so much in the character's comeuppance as in knowing that, in the end, karma's gonna getcha. I never think about her anymore, but when I do school visits, kids often ask me if I know what happened to Little Bad.

I do.

She had the nerve to try to friend me on social media.

I guess she doesn't remember her role in my middle school experience.

Whatever. What goes around comes around, and the social media picture of Little Bad's life is pretty sad.

And my life is now pretty awesome.

The other thing I hear a lot from both kids and adults is that they had (or have) a Little Bad in their life too. I find that so . . . frustrating. Generation after generation, despite what we try to do to curtail bullying in schools, Little Bads abound. But here's the good news: For us writers, they are the clay from which we can mold great villains.

So if you have (or had) a Little Bad in your life, change their name, change their hair color, and start raking them over the coals of a story. Every hero needs a villain to skewer. Have fun slow-roasting yours.

# 16

## SETTING

Where you set your story can be as important as the characters you put in it. In some instances, setting can be very much like a character, with its own style and mood and personality. And, as with your characters, your setting should be one with which you're very familiar.

If your story is set in a real or fictionalized version of a city or region (past, present, or future), what's on the page must at least approximate the reality. Authors might spend years really getting the feel of a place, the nuance of it, and smart authors will choose somewhere exciting or exotic, or immerse themselves in places with stunning landscapes, or those steeped in fascinating history.

Unfortunately, I didn't take the smart-author route. All of my books are set in places you *wouldn't* want to go. The bad part of town. Homeless camps. Hospitals. Dilapidated apartments.

Dementia care facilities. Barren stretches of desert. Spider-infested cellars . . .

When I started writing, I didn't consider cultivating knowledge about a setting apart from what I already knew. I didn't really consider setting at all. I just let what was around me work its way onto the page, and what was around me was mostly not pretty.

I lived with my husband in a tiny box of a rented house in Santa Maria, California. The Box House was near the intersection of Broadway and Main Street and a short walk from the Town Center Mall.

Also in the vicinity were St. Mary's Church, the Salvation Army, the police station, the fire station, city hall, the courthouse, lawyers' offices, and the library. A little farther away were a seniors-only apartment building, a seedy hotel, a just-as-seedy bar, and other random small businesses, including a corner store.

Sammy Keyes lives in a seniors-only highrise on the corner of Broadway and Main in the "fictional" town of Santa Martina. Near the highrise? A seedy hotel, a just-as-seedy bar, a corner store, the Town Center Mall, city hall, the police station, the fire station, the library, St. Mary's Church, and the Salvation Army.

The setting was easy to keep track of in my mind. It was easy to follow Sammy Keyes wherever she went because these were my stomping grounds. I could make them feel real on the page because they were real in my mind.

Every seedy detail.

When my husband and I moved into the Box House, the four hundred square feet seemed luxurious. We'd lived our first year together in a tiny duplex that had a single way in (and out) and a bedroom doorway that was half blocked by the refrigerator.

Moving gave us a second bedroom, so despite the structure's being a literal box, flat roof and all, we were grateful for the extra space and willing to spruce it up. We repainted the walls, replaced the carpet, refinished the cabinets, unstuck the windows, planted a lawn and shrubs, and built fences.

But as time would show us, there really is no polishing a turd. The roof leaked, the plaster peeled, the mold grew, the floor in the kitchen sagged as if it might collapse into the dirt cellar beneath it. Cats came to die (and decompose) by the floor heater under the house, and I swear the bugs were just letting us live there.

But worse than the decay surrounding us on the inside was what surrounded us on the outside.

Today, if you drive down the street where we lived, you would likely describe the neighborhood as quaint. It's in what's now called the Cottage District, and the houses in this area definitely have character, with no two being the same. But once we were living there, we got to know the neighborhood in a different way. We got to see the underbelly.

From the house across the street came regular shouting and screaming, which sometimes escalated into front-yard altercations, with police regularly zipping over from the station two blocks away to break up another round of domestic violence.

Behind us was a dirt alley that divided our street from the next one over. Designed for trash pickup, the alley was also the access point for shacks and converted garages that were rented to people living under the radar. This included drug dealers and gangbangers, who were clearly fond of punctuating the night air with gunshots.

Next to us on the west side was a little old man who'd had polio as a child and had no family to care for him. We helped him out but were told to keep away when a middle-aged man who saw an easy target moved in as his "caregiver." Before long, elder abuse was in full swing, something we could hear clearly, as our windows were only a narrow driveway apart. Our calls to the police yielded nothing but animus and threats from the "caregiver" because the old man was too afraid to press charges.

Around the corner was the Salvation Army, where home-less people congregated. It wasn't unusual to find a homeless person sleeping on our front porch in the morning or peeing in its sheltered corner at night.

Our plan was to work hard and save our pennies until we had enough for a down payment on our own place, and get out. When it was just my husband and me and the two big huskies, that plan seemed manageable.

Crowded, but manageable.

But when it was my husband and me, two big huskies, and two little kids, the plan began to crumble. At least, *I* began to crumble. "I am not spending another Christmas in this house!" became my annual refrain. There was no room to move, no space to bake, no spot for a tree, and with kids now, the tabletop variety was just not cutting it.

My sister likened living in our home to living in a submarine, and that was a pretty accurate description. Tables and chairs were folded up and tucked away when not in use. Things were stored under, behind, and over. My desk was a small secretary with a fold-down shelf, crammed against the wall at the foot of our bed. I sat on the edge of the mattress to use it.

Things went from tight to tighter, and despite my threats, Christmases continued to come and go. With kids in the picture, expenses grew and my patience shrank.

Nowhere in our plan was there a clause that said the move would take so long. If there had been, I would have come up with a different plan!

But day by day, week by week, year by year, time kept ticking. I wrote the first six Sammy Keyes books on a compact computer at that fold-down desk, letting the outside in as I sat on the edge of the bed.

The kids went from infants to toddlers to trike riders to bike riders. Santa brought bunk beds. Storage buckets stretched to the ceiling.

And then finally, *finally*, we moved.

Goodbye, Santa Maria!

But I couldn't actually fully leave. I might not have been living in Santa Maria anymore, but I returned to Santa *Martina* in my mind each day for the next fifteen years as I continued to write about Sammy Keyes. Sammy's world was undeniably a part of me, something that happened in a way I'd never intended, hadn't seen coming, and couldn't escape.

What's also undeniable is that, despite my protestations, I wouldn't trade those years in the Box House for anything, because that setting is what made Sammy who she is. Her world is steeped in underbelly. Her resourcefulness comes from *not* having things. When she's trapped by a gangster in a spider-infested cellar with little to work with to save herself or the kidnapped girl she's found there, I can picture exactly where she is. It's just like the cellar beneath the Box House kitchen. I know all about the creepy pull-up door, the water heater that's down there, all about the odds and ends coated with dirt, and the crawl space vent along the edge where you can see feet walking by outside.

I know exactly how icky and creepy and scared Sammy feels, trapped in that cellar.

I would like very much to forget that cellar.

And yet . . .

When I heard last year that the house was being demolished, I wanted to go. Not to watch, necessarily, more to say goodbye.

And it was weird. I got all emotional. It wasn't that I was romanticizing having lived there; it was more that this was the place where so much began. The porch held the memory of drug-addled vagrants and puddles of pee, sure, but it also held the mailbox.

The Hope-in-the-Mail mailbox.

And, with time and distance and the eighteenth and final Sammy Keyes book recently completed, I recognized how much living there had *given* me.

How much I'd learned and grown by being there.

How there might never have been a Sammy Keyes if I'd had the good fortune to live somewhere better.

What this has taught me is that your setting plays a crucial role in the creation of your characters. Where you place them influences who they are, what they experience, how they react, and who they become.

Also that no matter how great our plan is, there are things we can never fully escape, any more than we can escape ourselves. And maybe as writers we're actually *fortunate* to be in environments where the streets hiss with danger and characters lurk in the shadows.

So if you've experienced hard times, if you're having trouble getting through them or moving past them, try *using* them. See if there's something to be gained from them in both your creativity and your personal growth. Apply what you've been through to a fictional setting and to the creation of characters. Turn your pain and struggle into stories of resilience, compassion, and triumph.

Because the best way to truly get past hard times may be to look back on them with an eye toward what they've *given* you, as opposed to what they've taken.

# 17

# PET PIGS AND OTHER DISTRACTIONS

In theory, creating a detailed outline of your novel before you begin writing it is a smart, practical, efficient idea. It will keep your story on track, help guide you through the process, and get you where you plan to go.

Since I'm someone who loves a to-do list, it seems logical that I would also love detailed outlining.

I do not.

Not for novel writing, anyway.

I have tried it on several occasions in hopes that it would make the revision process easier, but I've found that a detailed outline (a) stifles my creativity and (b) takes a lot of the fun out of the actual writing. There's a sense of true excitement when you're submerged in the creation of a story and something totally unexpected pops up. It's that moment of transitioning from being at the helm of the story to being along for the ride.

For example, in a scene I was writing for the fifth Sammy

Keyes book (*Sammy Keyes and the Curse of Moustache Mary*), I knew Sammy and her friends were going to come upon a little old lady dressed in black who was walking along the side of the road. I knew the lady's name was Lucinda Huntley. I knew her Wild West backstory. I knew that she was on her way to crash the funeral of a lifelong foe.

What I did not know until the words appeared on the page was that Lucinda Huntley would be walking a two-hundred-pound pet pig.

A *pig?*

Hello?

What was a *pig* doing here? On the side of the road. With a tiny, hunched-over woman dressed in black.

I had no idea, but soon the pig had a name.

Penny.

And then the pig had a big black bow tied around her neck. And a personality. A snorty, intelligent, funny personality.

But . . . *why?* What was the pig going to do? What purpose did it serve?

I had no idea.

Still. I already *liked* the pig, so I threw caution to the wind and followed where it led.

Now, the danger of letting an unexpected pig nuzzle its way into your story is that it may lead you on a wild truffle chase. Or it may simply become a distraction with no real reason for being there. And the *problem* with that is that once you get to know the pig and have given it the chance to fall in love with the ornery cop in your story (which you find incomparably hilarious), it's hard to be objective about what the pig is actually contributing to the story.

And if it turns out that the pig *isn't* serving a purpose—if the pig starts to get in the way or you find yourself losing track of it—you must corral the thing and take a long, hard look at it. Because, come on, it's completely impractical for a little old lady to have a two-hundred-pound pet pig, and do you really want to get into why she has it or where it sleeps?

If not, good writing requires that you get rid of the pig.

Cut it out of the story.

Hello, bacon.

Which is a whole slab of work. Much more than if you'd never followed the pig in the first place.

But here's the thing about "going with the pig": It's fun. It's unexpected. It's exciting. Going with the pig puts joy in writing, and I highly recommend it *if* (and this is a big if) you're willing to edit out the pig when it becomes clear that it is not earning its keep in your story.

Fortunately, what I've found is that most of the time your subconscious will find ways to put that pig to work. I like to think there's a reason pigs show up in the first place, and that once I follow along for a bit, I'll understand what that reason is. In the case of Penny, she became an integral part of solving the mystery, and she was, in fact, such a well-loved character that she survived the entire series and showed up to embarrass Officer Borsch one last time in the final book.

In civilized circles, "going with the pig" is referred to as "organic writing." Some people also call it "pantsing," which is an adaptation of the old expression *flying by the seat of your pants,* which basically means you're actually kinda clueless about where your story's going and you're just following your characters wherever they lead. Writers are often asked, *Are you a plotter or a pantser?*

What I do is basically a balance of both. I may go with the pig, or have episodes of pantsing, but I'm also definitely a plotter, and in the end, furthering the plot (or contributing to character development) is going to win out over going hog-wild, stumbling after my characters wherever they may lead.

I call the hybrid of plotting and pantsing "signposting."

Signposting gives you something that's less than an outline and more than a blank page. Not only does it help get you where you're intending to go and allow for surprise developments, it also breaks the story into more manageable chunks.

Imagine you're taking a road trip from San Francisco to New York City. And let's say that after looking at the various choices, you decide to take a southern route. Not the fastest way, but you want to visit places you haven't been before. Your plan is to make it to the Arizona border by the end of your first day, then continue east, visiting Albuquerque, Oklahoma City, Memphis, and Richmond along the way.

Your destination is New York, but your first "signpost" is the Arizona border.

This is comparable to mapping out a (fairly linear) novel, where you plan the basic events that will take place in your story between the beginning and the end.

On your road trip (and metaphorically in your novel), what

you do not have plans for on the section of road (or writing) that runs between San Francisco and the Arizona border is the flat tire in Bakersfield, or getting trapped inside a truck-stop porta-potty in Barstow, or that crazy guy dressed in nothing but sandals who jumped onto your back bumper and cried, "Fweeee wiiiiide!"

You could not have planned for those things, and yet there they are, part of your cross-country adventure. Part of your story.

In writing, I plan my signposts. Usually, a signpost is the place I hope to get my characters to by the end of the chapter (with "place" being either destination or situation). Sometimes reaching it takes more time than that—maybe three chapters, depending on the organic writing that happens along the way. But regardless of crazy naked dudes on my bumper or pigs appearing out of nowhere, the goal is always to get to that signpost. And the goal of that signpost is to keep me on track toward my ultimate destination.

Now, as your story unfolds, you may find that you need to add—or subtract—signposts. That's okay. The trip is never going to go entirely as planned. And really, that's how you want it. It's the unexpected that keeps things interesting. So as you journey through your pages, keep one eye on the road and the other on your back bumper.

It's a great way to get from here to there.

# 18

## BEGINNING WITH THE ENDING

When a book is constructed without an ending in mind, it usually shows. Oh, the author can try patching things to cover it up after the fact, but it still shows. And sometimes it's just *bad*. Like paint sprayed over Bondo in the afternoon wind.

It's maddening to read a book that's great until the ending, where it just kind of fizzles. Or frays. Or leaves you feeling *meh*. Especially if it was *so good* up until then. When people talk about a book like that, they'll say how great it was, yadda-yadda, "but the author didn't know how to end it." And what's sad is, that disappointment is what they remember most about the story.

You don't want that to be your book. When you're excited about a story, there *is* a big temptation to get started on it before the ending's worked out. The writing devil on your shoulder will assure you that you'll figure it out when you get there. And maybe you will . . . but maybe you won't. In my opinion, knowing the ending is crucial. It's what you should be driving toward, and it, as your destination, affects (or should affect) everything else. It is worth the wait to figure it out ahead of time.

My most extreme personal experience with this was my book *Runaway*—the story about Holly Janquell, a girl who escapes abusive foster care, then lies, steals, and sneaks her way across the country.

Holly is the same homeless girl who appears in *Sammy Keyes and the Sisters of Mercy*. The one who Sammy discovered was living in a camouflaged cardboard box down by the riverbed. The same girl I was writing about when that homeless woman in a pink dress knocked on my door.

After *Sisters of Mercy* was published, a teaching colleague who read the book told me he wanted to know more about Holly. How did she come to be homeless and living on her own in that box?

My epiphany regarding backstory and fleshing out the history of the characters didn't kick in until I wrote *Sammy Keyes and the Runaway Elf*. So when I introduced Holly in *Sisters of Mercy*, all I really knew about her backstory was that her parents were dead and that she'd run away from bad foster care.

But now a fan of backstory, I liked the idea of exploring what Holly's life was like before she met Sammy. And the more I thought about her past, the more I wanted to give Holly her own book.

Regardless of where I began Holly's story, the ending should have been easy. It was already written in *Sisters of Mercy*. Holly is rescued by Sammy and becomes part of Sammy World.

But I didn't like that as the ending of *Runaway*. I thought

Holly should have her *own* ending, one centered on *her,* instead of Sammy's rescue. And the more I thought about it, the less I wanted to make an overt connection between Holly and Sammy. Holly's story wasn't about being rescued. It was about courage and determination and directing your own destiny and . . . I wasn't sure what all exactly, but I knew it had to be unique. It shouldn't look or sound or feel like a Sammy Keyes book.

But . . . how to accomplish that when all the signposts led to the rescue? Holly's future had already been established in Sammy World. And to be consistent, I couldn't deviate from what had happened to her in the series after the rescue.

So I liked the idea of telling Holly's story—actually, I found it gripping territory to explore—but I didn't love the ending.

And so I didn't begin writing.

I didn't stop *thinking* about it, however. *Years* went by. I wrote Sammy #5 and #6 and toyed with the idea that Holly's story could be told through journal entries. That would certainly set it apart from the structure of a Sammy Keyes book.

I wrote Sammy #7 and #8, where Holly's presence expands in Sammy World, and I found myself even more obsessed with her backstory. What had made her a journal writer? Could poetry—another structural departure from the Sammy Keyes series—be a part of it?

I wrote Sammy #9—*Psycho Kitty Queen*—in which Holly plays a big role and consequently occupied even more time in my mind. I was all in on her story being her journal. I was all in on including some poetry. But the ending. The darned ending. I still didn't have one I thought did *her* justice.

And then one day . . .

Which is always how it happens.

I was out on a run along a lovely dirt path that leads through groves of eucalyptus trees—a path where I often came upon a homeless person or two, a place where my mind naturally wandered to thoughts of Holly. And on this day, I was again thinking about her journal—where it had come from, how it had become her lifeline—when, *bam,* the ending hit me.

I stopped in my tracks and gasped, my eyes suddenly burning with tears. In the middle of the path, in the middle of the day, without any apparent reason, there I was, crying. (Which sounds melodramatic, I know, but any teacher who has read the book will completely understand this reaction.)

So there it was, seemingly out of the blue, the perfect ending.

And, just as unexpectedly, with the ending came the beginning. Because once I knew where I was going, I knew exactly how the story should start.

Finally, after more than six years of thinking about it, I was ready to write *Runaway.*

So, yes. I'm a believer in knowing your ending before you begin. Realistically, by the time you reach it, your ending won't be exactly as you envisioned it, or it will have shifted forward or backward on your story's timeline. But knowing what you're driving toward before you begin will contribute to your story becoming a tightly woven whole, and your readers will come away thinking and talking about story and theme and message, rather than a fumbled ending.

# 19

## THE INFAMOUS SAGGING MIDDLE

Jumping into a novel is fun. And when you're raring to go, it's easy. But how do you keep that energy flowing through the whole novel? How do you move forward if your story has lost its momentum?

The sagging middle is real. It's that place, midbook, where things begin to drag, where writers wait for an idea to come along to push them out of their rut. It's where many writers take an unproductive page-killing side trip in a desperate attempt to rev up their story.

When people—especially Sammy Keyes fans—began asking me how I'd learned tight plotting, the question caught me off guard because I'd never really analyzed what I do. The obvious thing to say was that I'd absorbed ideas about how to plot from all the reading I'd done. And I'm sure that's true. But I'd never dissected the structure of a book or tried to figure out what in the plotting of it made me want to keep turning the pages.

Well, except for chapter-ending cliff-hangers.

Cliff-hangers are awesome . . . and obvious.

But when I analyzed my own Sammy Keyes stories, it suddenly occurred to me that I'd picked up ideas about plotting from watching *Seinfeld*.

The *Seinfeld* sitcom had four main characters: Jerry, Elaine, George, and Kramer. In most of my favorite episodes, Elaine has her own story thread, as do George and Kramer, with Jerry being like a maypole that keeps the other characters tethered. There's a weaving of the various subplots, so the focus shifts from what's going on with Elaine, to George's awkwardness, to Kramer's quirky antics, with an occasional convergence in Jerry's apartment. And the very best episodes were the ones that wrapped up with all the story lines coming together to reveal a unifying theme or common thread.

Those very best episodes made my brain tingle with *Aha* and kept me coming back every week in hopes of another tightly braided adventure.

I gave this absolutely no analysis when I began writing about Sammy Keyes. But I can see now that the *Seinfeld* influence was definitely instrumental in my crafting the basic structure of each book in the series.

There's the apartment where Sammy lives with Grams, which is the pole tethering Sammy. It's the place where she feels loved and accepted and can hang out or hide out. But instead of the subplots following different characters around, we follow Sammy through three different strands of her life.

There's her home life, which includes living illegally in her grandmother's apartment, plus the dynamic of her family (not knowing who her dad is, being upset with her absentee mother, and unintentionally doing things to worry or upset her grandmother).

Then there's her school life, and the bubbling cauldron of anxiety that is middle school, including that wicked wasp of a girl, Heather Acosta.

And finally, there's the mystery. Out of all eighteen books in the series, only one central mystery takes place at school, so the mystery is what gets Sammy out and about, cruisin' the streets of Santa Martina on her skateboard, hiding in bushes, sneaking into the Heavenly Hotel, and getting trapped in spider-infested basements.

Weaving those three subplots (home, school, mystery) together creates a story line that has no room for a sagging middle. We move from the stressors of home, to what's happening at school, to Sammy gathering clues, without any "filler." One scene tags another, which tags another, all the way to the end, when they come together for the big finish.

So if you find your story starting to sag, consider adding a thread to work with. It's not possible to construct a plait with a single strand. You can twist it, but it won't hold. It's also hard to work with two strands. But three? Three's perfect. Once you get the hang of braiding with three, it moves along quickly and you'll find it to be self-supporting. (You can go for four, but four takes more finesse and can slow down the overall feel of your story.)

Some practical examples: If your main character is a kid, try giving them a job—dog walking, yard mowing, computer repair . . . something that gets them out of the rut of school and home. Or give them a passion for something. They can join a club, do public service, be on a sports or debate team.

For adult characters, give them an ailing parent they need to attend to periodically (or just a cranky one to visit). Or weave in a pet, or a child, or a neighbor, or a night class, or a gym membership (that they use), or the unexpected appearance of someone from their past. . . . The options are infinite.

I recommend this with the caveat that you don't just paste it in. It shouldn't be a strand that's over on the side, not woven into the whole of your story. It shouldn't just be an action for your main character to take; it must also set other action in motion. In other words, it can't be a drag on the story; it has to be there to propel the story along and, ideally, to support the theme.

Theme is key to the whole operation. It's the rubber band on the end of the braid. With it, everything stays tightly woven. Without it, the threads of your story may overlap, but they'll have a somewhat loose or frayed feeling.

So next, let's explore what theme is and the further merits of using one.

# 20

## THEME

So what *is* theme?

I had trouble grasping what teachers meant by *theme* when I was in school. It was a nebulous thing that always felt sort of esoteric and elusive. Not at all something I could analyze or memorize or even enjoy, like, say, the diagramming of sentences.

Turns out, theme is really not a hard concept to grasp. It's the Big Idea that umbrellas your story. And, ideally, its presence is felt but never stated. You might give it one mention to nudge focus that way, maybe two, but no preaching or teaching or interrupting-the-story-to-bring-you-this-very-important-message.

I have become a huge fan of theme. Often, it's the thing that makes me commit to writing a story. It's something *I* want to think more deeply about, something I want to delve into alongside my reader.

More than the exciting adventure or character growth, the theme is what I want the reader to be thinking about after the story is over. It's the concept they can apply to their own life, one that might help them in pursuit of their own personal happy ending. Or something to help them sort through their feelings, or assist them with how to react to or endure situations that may arise in their future by providing a mental trial run.

Please don't mistake theme for message.

Everyone hates overt "message" books, and that includes kids, who can smell them from across the library. If you're contemplating writing for children or teens, do not (do NOT) tell them what they should think, or what they should do, or how they should feel.

Instead, offer them food for thought—something to chew on after the book is done.

For a practical example of using theme, let's do a quick analysis of how the three threads of *Sammy Keyes and the Runaway Elf* are unified by its theme of embracing forgiveness.

1.  *Mystery:* For all the suspects Sammy follows in an effort to solve this story's mystery, the culprit turns out to be someone who'd grown vengeful because of the victim's unwillingness to forgive her for something she'd done years before.
2.  *School:* Bad-girl Heather's sneaky actions early in the book result in huge embarrassment for Officer Borsch. He doesn't know who's behind it, but when cornered by Sammy near the end of the book,

Heather breaks down and begs Officer Borsch to help and forgive her.

3. *Home:* Nosy neighbor Mrs. Graybill winds up in a nursing home. At first Sammy's like, *Good riddance,* because the woman has been on a relentless mission to prove Sammy's living at the Senior Highrise illegally. But then the bedridden Mrs. Graybill won't stop with her agonizing sounds, and what she's moaning and groaning about is wanting to see Sammy Keyes.

Which makes absolutely no sense.

She hates Sammy!

But she won't shut up, so when Sammy finally visits her, what comes out is Mrs. Graybill's backstory and why she grew into being such a bitter old woman, along with deathbed regrets about it. And what she begs for now is Sammy's forgiveness.

So we have separate threads that touch on the theme and crisscross each other throughout the book. And the rubber band at the end that holds them tightly together is Sammy's epiphany that in order to not become a bitter person like Mrs. Graybill, or wind up like the culprit, or even like Heather Acosta, she has to find a way to forgive her mother for the things she's done.

Sammy's takeaway brings the theme into sharp focus, but it does so in an organic way, without sermonizing.

The cool thing about being in tune with theme is that as

your story unfolds, you can find ways to incorporate it in places you didn't foresee. You can also go back during the revision process and shore it up.

So what's the Big Idea behind the story *you're* writing? What is it you're trying to convey or explore? What's your purpose for writing the book? Even if your purpose is simply "entertainment" or crafting a "story about nothing," a theme can create satisfying cohesiveness. And if you define your theme and write with it in mind, you'll find that opportunities for weaving it in will present themselves and that your overarching story line will be tighter and stronger for it.

And if you're writing to explore—to dig more deeply into a subject or emotions (or the ever-elusive meaning of life)—watch for a theme to develop. Because it will, and when it does, you can go back and reinforce it in the revision process to make it feel like it was there all along.

---

# 21

# HIDDEN ARCHITECTURE

Aside from the words you use on the page, there are lots of ways you can create a vibe or mood for your story by manipulating how and where you choose to place those words. A great example of that is a story told in free verse. You know, where an author . . .

*Takes a thought*
*And breaks*
*It*
*Into lines that*
*Flow*
> *and tumble and*
>> *fall*
*Down*
> *the*
>> *page.*

Free verse can be very dramatic. It can also feel like the author totally cheated, turning a fifty-page manuscript into three hundred artsy-fartsy choppy pages.

The decision to use free verse should be made for its contribution to the storytelling, not as a way to appear cool. Or pad pages. And *all* decisions you make on where to place or how to break your words should be done with the big picture in mind. Ask yourself: *Does it improve the telling of my story?*

Sometimes simple is better, and if that's the case, get out of your own way.

And sometimes artsy really does contribute, so if that's the case, use it.

My first novels were written with the straightforward structure of even-length chapters. It was the style I was most familiar with, and once *Sammy Keyes and the Hotel Thief* was written that way, the die was cast for the entire series.

*Flipped,* too, was written in standard chapters, but here the point of view switches chapter by chapter, with each of the two main characters telling their side of the story.

Then, when considering ways to write Holly's story in *Runaway,* I settled on the journal format, with touches of poetry throughout, to give it a structure very different from the Sammy Keyes books.

With the Shredderman books, I wrote with an eye toward white space on the page to appeal to and encourage kids who were becoming independent readers—something I will expand upon later.

But here I want to focus on the structure of *The Running*

*Dream* because I think it's a good example of what considered structure can contribute to the telling of a story, even when the reader doesn't recognize it's there.

To set things up, here are the pertinent basics:

*Story premise:* Jessica, a star high school runner, loses her leg in a horrible accident and feels like her life is over.

*POV:* First person.

*Takeaway:* Sometimes the finish line is actually a new starting line.

The story opens with Jessica in the hospital after the accident/amputation. The sentences—her thoughts—are short. Choppy. Incomplete. The whole first section is that way, and it's done in an effort to capture the feeling of breathlessness. Have you ever had a panic attack? That. Terror and racing heart and the inability to breathe . . . all of that is projected to the reader with the assistance of structure.

Then, as Jessica adapts to her new reality, the sentences lengthen. So do the paragraphs. Her thinking and her view of the world change and expand, and this is reflected in the easing flow of the language.

Most readers don't even notice the specifics of this because, like Jessica's recovery, it's gradual. But they *feel* it as they move through the pages, catching their own breath along the way.

More obvious in this book is the use of sections. Sections are commonly used to signal a change in time or location or narrative viewpoint. They help introduce a shift that's difficult to achieve with a segue or chapter break.

In *The Running Dream*, each section begins with its own chapter one . . . because in anything hard, you have to go back to the beginning, pull yourself together, and try again.

What's not so obvious in *The Running Dream* is the underlying purpose of the section breaks. There are five of them: "Finish Line," "Headwind," "Straightaway," "Adjusting the Blocks," and "Starting Line."

They represent a race run backward.

They represent that sometimes a finish line is actually a new starting line.

And the choice of five sections?

That's for the five stages of grief.

I don't expect every reader to pick up on this, and that's okay. It's more like a backdrop to the action onstage—once it's noticed, it becomes clear how much it contributes, but even if it's overlooked, it affects the experience of reading the story.

So think about different ways you might reinforce your story through structure. There is absolutely nothing wrong with straightforward chapters—if that's what works best for your story, don't mess with it. But there's no harm in considering alternate or supplemental ideas, and you may hit on something that contributes—even as unseen support—to the power of your story.

# 22

## DIALOGUE

Dialogue is the vocalization of your characters' thoughts. What your characters say helps to show us who they are. It's the way we begin to really hear them. Dialogue contributes to the creation of "voice," and it can make or break the reader's engagement with a book.

I have plenty to say about dialogue—which I'm happy to share—but really I think it comes down to this:

Listening.

I can write in a believable teen voice because I was surrounded by teens as a teacher, and also by my kids and their friends. I've been submerged in the teen voice for decades, and for decades, I've listened.

I've also taken notes. I'm not a big note-taker, but sometimes a real person will say something in a unique way that can spark a departure from my own known speech patterns and lead me to a new, fresh voice. I used to tell myself that I'd remember the syntax or turn of phrase, only to have it escape me half an hour later. So I've learned the hard way—it's better to jot it down.

I do not keep a three-by-five card in my back pocket. I've tried that and I've failed.

I'm also terrible at taking notes on my phone.

And a notebook?

Where did I put that again?

So unfortunately, I don't have a magic system to share, but I will say this: Just get it down. In whatever way works for you, jot it down.

You may be the organized sort and transfer it directly to a folder when you get home.

I would admire you greatly for that.

And, yeah, hate you a little too.

But if you're more like me, you may scribble it down and forget about it. Or lose it. Because maybe the kids are crying or school is stressing you out or you've trapped a burglar in your basement and he's screaming stuff at you that's more pressing than that clever turn of phrase you jotted down on a napkin at the coffee shop (not to mention that said burglar is spewing stuff your writer's brain is dying to also jot down if it weren't for the pesky need to dial 911).

So your little coffee shop note gets pushed aside and out of mind. But then, a week, a month, six months later, you rediscover that note in a jacket pocket. And in the interim a character has developed in your mind or on the pages of your project, and you realize that the phrase or syntax has been lurking in your subconscious, and that you're ready to use it . . . or maybe you already have.

The act of writing things down helps us remember, even if we think we've forgotten.

The point is to tune in and pay attention to the language of others. It doesn't take much of a twist to give a character a unique sound, something that can be done quite simply by giving them a signature phrase or expression—one you may have heard in that coffee shop one morning.

For example, in *Flipped*, Bryce uses ". . . and that, my friend, was . . ." That's *his* phrase. His friends don't use it, Juli certainly doesn't, nor do his parents or teachers or anybody else in the book. That is *his*, and it helps separate his voice from Juli's as we alternate between their points of view.

Part of "listening" transfers to listening to your characters. So if one of them pops off with "Dude!" (or some such), do not muddy the voices by having other characters use that expression. Sure, in real life, no one teen in a group is going to have an exclusive on that (or any other) expression, but if you're looking to help define your characters through dialogue, it's very helpful to have expressions or phrases that are specific to them.

Sammy Keyes uses "holy smokes."

Nobody else in Sammy World does.

Sammy's friend Dot uses funny expressions based on her Dutch heritage. Only Dot would say something like "Whirling windmills!" when expressing her surprise.

And Sammy's friend Holly uses "crud."

Nobody else in *Runaway* or Sammy World ever does.

The benefit of this is when you're constructing dialogue and you want it to move quickly, without the drag of attribution (specifying who's saying what), you could do this:

"Holy smokes!"
"Whirling windmills!"
"Oh, crud."

There are *no* attributions, but there is no doubt about who's speaking.

The danger with signature phrases is the tendency to overuse them. It's best to think of them as a spice. Something to sprinkle into your dialogue. If you oversalt (or -pepper or -paprika), you will ruin the dish. So how much is too much? This is best assessed in the revision process, rather than trying to gauge it in real (writing) time. Maybe you weren't aware that you'd used a particular phrase four times in five pages because it took you all day to write those five pages. But when it takes seven minutes to read those five pages, you'll realize that you've oversalted. Fortunately, the dish isn't ruined, because you can easily excise. When in doubt, cut it out.

Another way I've learned to avoid the drag of attributions (which also helps curb the use of *-ly* adverbs) is to marry a character's actions to their words. For example:

Dot was panting when she reached us. "He's . . . not . . . there!"

I yanked her behind the fence. "Then where?"

Holly pointed at a man hurrying toward us from across the street. "Uh . . . we might want to get out of here?"

That's a little overdone, but it gives you the idea of how coupling action and attitude with dialogue can convey a lot, and quickly.

There's also the technique of giving a character a "signature item." For example, Sammy wears high-tops. Torn-up, secondhand high-tops. And Dot's drink of choice is (ugh) root beer.

So instead of writing something like *"I'm not doing that,"* *Dot said angrily,* you can convey motion, attitude, and personality by replacing it with *Dot slammed down her root beer. "I'm not doing that."*

In all of the above examples, you can add *and said* before the quote, or tack on a *she said* after it, but why? We're going for action and forward motion. Adding the attribution is unnecessary and counterproductive.

Likewise, when Sammy finds herself in trouble with authority—at home, at school, or at the police station—we might find her toeing the ground with her high-top or stepping with one toe on the peeling rubber of the other. This creates the feeling of remorse or nervousness without her having to say that's how she's feeling. *"It wasn't me," I told him nervously* gets the boost of both motion and emotion (plus added detail about the location) when we script it as *I toed at a crack in the linoleum. "I swear it wasn't me."*

As with any writing device, don't overdo it or move beyond transparent. If your character adjusts their hat or twirls their hair or blows their nose too often, they will become a caricature of themselves—something you definitely don't want. *He said* and *she said* are often the cleanest and most transparent way to create dialogue. If it fits your style to sometimes substitute *said* with verbs like *cackled* or *panted* or *cajoled,* go for it—sparingly. Just avoid at all costs redundant or overdone attributions like *cackled derisively* or *panted breathlessly* or *cajoled pleadingly.* If the verb doesn't cut it on its own, find a better verb.

So, in crafting believable dialogue, *listen* both to the people around you and to your characters. Speak a character's words aloud and ask yourself: *Does it sound real?* If it doesn't ring true, start whittling. People usually don't talk in long, convoluted sentences. For snappy dialogue, avoid getting too clever or long-winded. Your character may simply be trying to say "Dude, no." If that's the case, don't say more. Say that.

And try finding something unique about your characters—a mannerism, an expression, a clothing style . . . anything. Then challenge yourself to write some dialogue with limited attributions and no -*ly* adverbs. See if it helps the back-and-forth between characters come to life. Now, too much back-and-forth between characters without attributions can become confusing to the reader, so don't go crazy—to achieve a good flow, you'll need to keep fine-tuning the exchange until it reads smoothly.

It takes a little effort, but as your dialogue starts to really come alive, you'll see that it's worth it.

# 23

# WRITING CHOPS

It is imperative that you keep in mind who your audience is. If you're writing for adults, try a highbrow literary style if you like—many truly enjoy it.

But if you're writing for kids, too much complex or convoluted language can be off-putting or, worse, sound phony. It can also really detract from forward movement in a story as the reader wades through description on their quest for action.

Around our house we use an expression to describe a rock song that has a lot of speedy guitar work. We say it has too much weedle-lee-woo. If a guitar player is shredding away—notes flying, with hammer-ons and pull-offs galore—but it doesn't take the song anywhere, that's too much weedle-lee-woo. Sure, the player has great chops, but the way they're being applied is not actually contributing to the musicality of the song. He or she is just showing off, and it doesn't take long for the listener to become bored (or make cracks about weedle-lee-woo).

But a tasty guitar lick slipped in between phrases can add a *lot* to a song. It can totally *make* a song.

The same thing applies to the writing of books. Too much weedle-lee-woo and the reader begins to fast-forward or tune out. Especially for kids, long, detailed description without action is the kiss of death. If you're going to write lengthy paragraphs about the beauty of the ocean as it cascades onto the waiting shore and glistens in the shimmering moonlight, you'd better throw in some sharks quick or your book and all its beautiful words are going to get sidelined.

In a nutshell: Don't try to impress your reader with your writing chops. Throw in a few tasty literary licks and get back to the story.

Of course, it's possible to go too far the other way. A book that is all plot without the grace of beautiful language or the beating heart of compelling characters is like a movie that is nonstop action. Things may be exploding and crashing and shooting and crumbling all over the place, and the intention is likely to keep viewers on the edge of their seats, but the result is that our senses get numbed and we stop caring. Aliens invade, civilizations crumble, scores of people die . . . yet we don't *feel* anything.

If the plot is all action, viewers—and readers—have no time to process anything more than forward movement. There's no opportunity to get inside the heart of the characters. We need time to come down a little so the next shock actually affects us.

It's a balance. And your job as a writer is to create the *right* balance for the story you want to tell and the audience you want to reach. That might mean going heavier on the literary licks, or it might mean intensifying the plot.

So definitely work on your chops, but also spend time analyzing when they add, when they detract, and when they, you know, weedle-lee-woo.

· III ·

# BEING A WRITER

## 24

## BECOMING A FINISHER

Writers write. They don't just dream about doing it or rationalize why they aren't able to at the moment; they face the blank page and they write.

So how do you make that happen? How do you transition from thinking about it or dabbling in it to really *doing* it?

Setting the alarm for five in the morning doesn't guarantee you'll actually get up then. It's much easier to turn off the alarm and go back to sleep.

I am a big fan of sleep.

And telling yourself *Today could be the day* will not get you out of bed either, because whatever project you're working on has more to do with the future than the present.

And right now, sleep is so . . . *nice.*

When people began asking me how I managed to drag myself out of bed day after day for something that didn't seem to be working out for me, I started questioning it myself.

Part of the answer may lie in my upbringing. My parents immigrated to the United States from the Netherlands (often referred to as Holland). Known for its tulips and windmills, it's also home to one of the Seven Wonders of the Modern World—the Zuiderzee Works, which is a man-made system of dams and dikes used to reclaim land from the sea. After centuries of repeated flooding and devastation that wiped out whole villages, the Dutch engineered a way to hold back the sea and convert a thousand square miles of submerged territory into useful land.

So somewhere in the mind-set of Dutch people is the notion that you can go up against huge forces of nature. That you can push back the sea. That you can rise up from disaster, rebuild, and flourish.

That requires a strong work ethic, which my parents definitely had and firmly impressed upon us kids. We had a checklist of chores, and we did them. And when we were done, Mom always had something else for us to do.

Our parents believed in living within their means and saving for a rainy day (and it rains a lot in Holland). Their approach to all things was built on the precept that if you could do it yourself, you did it, and if it was something you didn't know how to do yet, you figured out how.

Also, we didn't waste. Dinner was finished or it became breakfast. Clothes were handed down. Things were mended, repaired, or repurposed. We rarely went out to eat.

Sandwiched between brothers, I was not given special treatment for being a girl. I did learn the domestic skills that girls were expected to have back then—sewing, cooking, cleaning—but I also did the things my brothers did, like chopping wood, moving wheelbarrows of dirt, laying bricks, hammering nails . . . that sort of thing.

There was no going out to play until the job was done, and done didn't just mean the task was complete. It also meant that the work area was swept up and the tools were put away.

I'm certain I'm a "finisher" because of the way my parents raised me. Starting something and *not* finishing it feels weird to me. Knowing something's not done sort of *bugs* me.

When I started my first novel, I didn't really know what I was doing. Nobody but my husband knew I was writing it and there was no deadline, so as the reality of the *work* necessary to write a novel sank in, it would have been completely reasonable to put it aside.

But 627 pages later, I finished it.

And even if it was pretty terrible, that doesn't matter. Sometimes finishing is accomplishment enough. The sheer will it takes to get to that last page gives you the confidence that you can, in fact, do this, and the bonus is that the next time you begin writing, you'll be a stronger, better, more confident writer.

It's like running a marathon when you've never done it. You set the goal, you do the training, you get to the starting line, and the only thing—the *only* thing—that matters is getting over the finish line. Sure, you start out with your lofty goals, but in the end your pace doesn't matter, your splits don't matter, your overall time doesn't matter . . . all that matters is crossing that finish line.

There are always great excuses to quit (and your brain will play tricks on you and conjure up doozies beginning around Mile 18). But getting over the finish line of your first marathon—even if you come in last—will change your life. Everyone I know who's done it has said the same thing: It gives you the belief, way down inside, that you can do anything.

Writing your first novel is very much like running your first marathon. Finish it and you'll know you can, which is *huge*.

So what's the harm in quitting and trying again with a new idea?

Quitting breeds doubt. It also keeps you from flexing your writing muscles. Writing to completion will strengthen your skills. Beginnings are easy. Endings are awesome. But to get from the beginning to the end, you need to traverse the middle, and yes, there'll be a Mile 18 in your novel.

The middle is where books can begin to drag. It's where most writers lose their steam. How are you going to get good at mitigating the sagging middle if every time you reach it, you quit? Becoming a finisher isn't hard, it's just habit. And you can set that habit with everyday things. Fold the laundry, *put it away*. Vacuum your room, *put the cleaner away*. Do the homework, *put it in your backpack*.

The trick is to keep the tasks small and manageable so you can say, *I finished*. If you're tackling a big job—something like painting a room—divide it into manageable subtasks. Instead of "paint the room," make it "prep the room," then "mask the room," *then* "paint the room." Finishing each step gets the job done, and it doesn't feel so overwhelming.

Apply the concept of finishing small steps to your writing: Finish the page. Finish the chapter. Repeat until you've finished the story.

Step by step.

Page by page.

Don't let your mind trick you into quitting.

You can do this.

# 25

## REVISION AS ARCHENEMY

Over a year after I'd been invited via a personally signed but boilerplate postcard to submit *How I Survived Being a Girl* to an editor, her rejection letter landed in my mailbox.

So much time had passed that a response from her was unexpected, but it was a nice rejection in that it wasn't the typical badly copied version of an ancient ditto from the sixties that said the usual *We're sorry, this is not right for us at this time.* (And yes, some rejections I received did look that overcopied and outdated.)

Instead, it was a full-page typed letter that contained "some comments and suggestions" that she "hoped would be helpful." She gave some general input on improving structure and character growth, but I could not really see past her comment about the book's length.

"It needs to be about half as long."

*What?*

I tossed her letter aside.

Another rejection. And it had taken her a year to write it! So, *pffft*.

But my husband had a different reaction. "This is actually a really nice letter," he said.

I scowled at him. *Pffft*.

"Maybe you should consider some of what she said?"

"She wants me to cut it in half!"

"Maybe start by looking it over with her letter in mind?"

"I'm not going to cut it in half!"

I remember heated silence. Mostly generated by me. And then . . .

"Wendelin, this is a real letter from a real editor. If you ever want to get published, you might want to consider what she has to say!"

"But . . . cut it in *half*?"

It took a few days, but I finally did sit down and look at the manuscript. And with so much time having passed since I'd written it—and with substantially more writing experience now under my belt—I grudgingly recognized the truth in her objections. The plot *did* meander. The structure *was* mushy.

But still. Cut it in *half*?

How was I ever going to do that?

I read through the manuscript several times, then finally rolled up my sleeves and started hacking. Whole chapters came out. I trimmed wherever I could. I streamlined the story and focused on tighter writing.

I also fudged the margins a tad (the opposite of what we do

when trying to meet a page requirement in school) and worked to get each chapter that ended on a mostly empty page consolidated so the text was pulled up enough to eliminate a page. I combined paragraphs, excised words to save a line, changed the kerning of a few words to compress.

Yes, I cheated!

But I also removed huge chunks, added structure, and worked hard at eliminating unnecessary or overdone language.

I started with a manuscript that was just under three hundred pages. The revision I submitted three months later was "about half," sneaky margins and all.

This was my first real experience with revision.

I hated it.

When I heard back from the editor again, she thanked me for the revision and said she'd been getting favorable responses to the manuscript from people in-house. Then she hinted at what was to come: "I think it will probably need one more revision (not as drastic as the first!) but it's very close and I'm optimistic about its future."

A year and four months later, I received my first editorial letter for the book, which had finally been bought by her publishing house. It was three solid, single-spaced pages of "lots of little and one big thing" that I needed to work on.

I came to hate revising even more. I was sick of looking at this story. And she wanted me to take more parts out? And then *add* at the end? Why couldn't we just go with it as it was? Why couldn't it just be a book already?

But I'd signed a contract and I was committed, so after a

few days of grumbling, I got back to work. I sent the revision to her with a letter outlining the changes I'd made . . . and reasons for the ones I hadn't. And the truth is, I was fine with the end result, but getting there had been hard. Really hard. Once your story is branded in your brain a certain way, it's hard to erase that impression. Changing it takes time and a willingness to step back.

I wasn't very good at that yet.

And although I could see the improvement the revision had made, I still more-than-kinda hated the process.

And we weren't done yet. In the next rounds of back-and-forth, the manuscript would become so marked up and messy that at one point I retyped the entire thing. I was developing a style of switching between past and present tense—something you'll find in the Sammy Keyes series—but had not mastered it yet. So in the end, the editor put her foot down about my switching-tenses style, threw *Girl* entirely into past tense, and explained that she was giving it over to a copy editor, who would "focus on grammar, punctuation, spelling—the more technical aspects of writing."

So, wait. We were going to go through it *again*?

Yes. Again and again and again and *again*. By the time *Girl* was an actual book, revision had become my new archenemy.

It took me *years* to finally understand that revision is actually a writer's best friend.

## 26

## REVISE, RINSE, REPEAT

Hindsight being what it is, I look back on the ten years of rejection and see that I could have helped myself tremendously if I had caught the revision bug earlier. My MO for those ten years was to write something, read it through a couple of times for errors or clunky sentences, and call it done. So the formal revision process for *Girl* was quite a shock, and when it was over, I was just glad to be done with it. Enough already.

But the process began all over again with Sammy Keyes. At one point, before any of the four Sammy Keyes books I'd written were picked up, my now-official editor suggested that maybe Sammy's story really began with the second title, *Skeleton Man*.

As in, dump the whole first book.

Which felt miserably like "cut it in half and I'll look at it again." But no fudging of margins was going to get me to the next phase this time. It felt like she was close to making an offer on Sammy, which suddenly was scary. I had to figure out a way to save *Hotel Thief.*

In the several years it had taken me to write those first four Sammy Keyes books—*Hotel Thief, Skeleton Man, Sisters of Mercy,* and *Runaway Elf*—I had never gone back to read any of them. And now, poring over the manuscript for *Hotel Thief,* I was kinda shocked. The writing was . . . rough. The plotting was . . . uneven. And Sammy wasn't entirely . . . Sammy.

Oh.

*But,* I thought, *I can fix this.*

The way to become a better writer is to write. You want to become a better painter? Paint. You want to become a better ballplayer? Shoot hoops. You want to become a shreddin' guitar player? Spend a lot of time with your instrument.

Writing is deceptive because it feels like something we already know how to do. After all, we've been writing since elementary school. But the craft of writing is just like everything else—the more you practice, the better you get.

So the unforeseen benefit of it taking for-stinkin'-ever to place the Sammy Keyes books was that while I was hoping for a contract on *Hotel Thief,* I'd kept writing, building up four books' worth of pages. Without even realizing it, I'd become a much stronger writer. Suddenly the chance to save *Hotel Thief* seemed like an opportunity rather than a chore. And in addition to improving the writing, I was now able to create better continuity in the series' evolving story line. There were things that happened in *Runaway Elf* that could be seeded in *Hotel Thief*. There was character growth from book to book that I could now set up better.

And then there was the writing. Because of my general ignorance about craft, I didn't realize that my style of switching between past and present tense was Just Not Done. A book was either past tense or present tense. You didn't go back and forth. But I was trying to capture the way teens talk, and what they do is switch tenses. *I was at the store with my mom and we were just going down the aisle, minding our own business, when all of a sudden out of nowhere this guy jumps in front of us and says, "Let me use your phone!"*

That goes from past to present and it feels really natural, but it is, or at least was, a literary no-no.

Well, I didn't know-know that. Not until the tense (and, at times, *tense*) debate over *Girl*—an argument that I'd lost. And even when I *did* know-know, I didn't want to give it up with Sammy. It had become so much *her* style. It made her feel real—like any one of the kids I saw every day.

In order to not lose to convention again, I needed to get better at it. Make the tense transitions smoother. Find a way to make it really flow.

With all that in mind, I dug into *Hotel Thief*. And, tense issue aside, it turned out to be a major overhaul.

Ugh!

But after I got past the initial feeling of being overwhelmed, after I'd done a new rough draft of the entire book and was back to the beginning and starting again, after the fear was gone and the mission was clear, I realized with a wave of disbelief that I was enjoying myself.

*Say! I like green eggs and ham! I do!*

And instead of wondering why the whole publishing process had to take so long, I was relieved to be able to revisit my work. Having the opportunity to go back to the beginning of Sammy's story suddenly felt like a gift.

And what a gift. *Sammy Keyes and the Hotel Thief* launched the series by winning an Edgar—a very prestigious award for mystery writers—and I'm certain it wouldn't have if it had come out in its original form.

So now, except for the rush I get from writing an exceptionally good scene, or the relief of typing the final page of a novel, revision has become my favorite thing in the process. And I no longer wait for the end to revise. I do it as I go, in a sort of forward-looping manner. I'll write a chapter, rewrite the chapter, put it aside. I'll repeat that for three or four chapters, then go back to the beginning and read through all the chapters, revising as I go, adding or subtracting little things to support what's happened in the story since the newest section was written. Then I'll move forward, writing the next few chapters, looping back to the beginning, reading the entire thing, revising to support new developments. I do this for the entire book, then put it aside for a week or so while I bask in the glory of the last line of a new book.

By basking, I mean I clean house, pay bills, do all those

things I've been neglecting since I came down with finish fever—something that always hits when I reach the last stretch of a book.

Then I go back to the very beginning, read the manuscript with fresh eyes and a red pencil, and have at it.

And boy, do I make a mess!

The pages get bloodied and slashed, paragraphs are lassoed and arrowed to different pages, redundancies are removed, sections are bracketed for possible axing, paragraphs are clarified, and bits (usually the funny bits) are added.

It takes weeks, that first time through. And once the changes are (deciphered and) entered, I print the pages and begin again.

Then I enter the new changes and begin again.

And do it all again.

And again.

And *again*.

When I think I'm done, I give the manuscript to my husband to read. Because he is an accomplished writer and I trust him to give me honest feedback, he is the only person who sees my work at this stage. After he goes through it with a red pen, catching mistakes both big and small, we discuss.

Then I have at it once more, keeping in mind his comments and suggestions. When I'm done with that, I print and read and revise again.

And again.

And *again*.

And every time, I find something to change, something to tighten, clarify, add, or subtract.

And then finally, after maybe twenty or thirty total cycles, I read through it and find that I've changed nothing—or at least very little.

If the book delves into a subject or skill that's new to me, or if it includes a culture that is not my own, it's at this point that I'll ask an expert—usually someone I've been working with during the creation of the story—to read the manuscript.

Next I revise and polish the story with their feedback in mind, and *that's* when I finally submit it to my editor, knowing full well that she will return it to me with suggestions on ways to improve it.

It took me a long time to realize that writing is what's fun for the author, but revising is what makes what we've written enjoyable for the reader.

Revision is not spell-checking.

Revision is not fine-tuning punctuation.

Revision is at least as important as the initial writing. It takes effort to make words flow together, to have paragraphs segue smoothly, to construct chapters that propel the reader forward. It takes effort to make the book an authentic, integrated entity, and, as painful as it may seem at first, the only way I know to get there is through dedicated, thoughtful revision.

No pain, no gain.

So learn to love it.

# 27

---

# WRITER'S BLOCK

The most common concern I hear from aspiring writers is that their story loses steam. They *do* know where they're going, they *were* off to a firecrackin' start, but . . . they're just *stuck*.

Blocked.

And kinda depressed about it.

"Do you ever get writer's block?" they ask.

I used to joke, "I don't have *time* for writer's block!" Not with a full-time job and little kids and a household to run. But looking deeper, I think what made me not feel blocked was the fact that I *didn't* have a lot of time to sit down and write. I had way more time away from the blank page than with it, but what was key to my not becoming blocked was that I used this time to think about what I *should* write when I had a chance to get back to it.

Probably the single most valuable tip I can give you about writing is this: When you're not at the keyboard, train yourself to think about your story, and only your story. This takes some corralling of your thoughts—and they will try to escape to sweeter pastures—but once you harness your thoughts and train them to stay on your story, you will be amazed by how much writing you can accomplish away from your desk.

You will have to give up some things to do this. TV, podcasts, other books . . . anything with a plot that your brain is attracted to. Because your creative mind will try to puzzle out what happens next on your favorite shows. It will be hijacked by fascinating podcasts. It is satisfied to read *someone else's* well-crafted story. Our brains like to figure things out, so don't give yours any options. Give it only your story, your plot, your problem to work on.

This is a silent process, and it's one that can be easily interrupted, so you have to keep forcing your thoughts back to your story, your plot, your problem.

When I'm working on a book and have a long road trip to take, I don't listen to music or audiobooks.

I force my brain to work on my story.

Just thinking about the characters, their relationships, their situation will create little scenes in your mind. Likely, no brilliant plot development will spring up right away, but don't be discouraged. Keep adding new ingredients, new ideas. Sprinkle in "what-ifs." It's okay to go a little wild.

Say your story needs something, so you imagine in a dog. You see your main character now owning a dog and all that entails (no pun intended). But that seems a little generic, so you let go of the harness on your thoughts and imagine instead that the pet is a snake. A large snake that has free rein in the house. No, wait. Beyond the house. It accompanies your main character on shopping expeditions . . . it's that kind of snake.

Which means your character is now that kind of person.

And what if your character gets tangled up in a jewelry heist (you can figure out the details of that later) and the snake . . . the snake somehow manages to swallow a priceless Fabergé egg—not because the snake's a thief, but because it's hungry. And when your character escapes the melee (with the pet snake, of course), they unwittingly make off with an invaluable treasure.

Okay. That's how you drive from Salinas to San Jose without realizing it.

You get lost in the heist.

You get lost in seeing the scene.

Now, you may wind up tossing the scene out the window, but you'll begin a new one or segue to an exploration of some, uh, *gem* from the tossed scene. And if you stay in your story long enough, eventually (and like magic) there'll be a *ding*, and a fully baked, absolutely delicious idea will pop out of your mental oven.

Doing this during a task that doesn't require much thought works best. It should be one that distracts part of your brain enough to allow the creative part of it to roam. Like folding the laundry, or washing the dishes, or scrubbing, well, anything. I can get so much "writing" done in an afternoon of window washing, it's amazing. And a job that generates white noise adds a layer of concentration, which is why driving (in little or no traffic) works. The hum of road noise is enough to create a cone of concentration. Other things that work really well are vacuuming, or mowing grass, or the classic (but ecologically wasteful) taking of a long shower.

When I'm writing a book, I live that book in my mind. When I'm jogging, when I'm driving, when I'm chore-ing, when I'm flying, when I'm falling asleep at night . . . I tune my brain in to my story.

You give up a lot to do this, but it works, and you can always binge-watch/listen/read after your book is written.

Well, unless you're like me, and you're already thinking about the next one.

# 28

# A LITTLE ABOUT RESEARCH

No matter what your story is about, research is likely to play a role in the writing of it, and real research requires more than looking things up in books or on the internet. You need to get physical.

I actually love the research part of writing a book. I didn't used to. It used to feel like an impediment to getting pages typed. And I found it difficult to ask strangers to help me figure things out.

It's tempting to fake it or fudge it or try some end run around it, but don't. Maybe a lot of readers won't notice, but for those who do, the book will be ruined. And you, as the author, will have let them down.

Let's say there's a book featuring a rock band of rookie musicians. Let's say the author has the entire band and their gear traveling to a gig in a Volkswagen van. Let's say the band arrives at the venue and the singer plugs her microphone into the power strip.

Most people would go along with that scenario, but anyone who has actually been in a rock band knows that the band and their gear cannot fit in a VW van. They will also know that plugging a microphone into a power strip is impossible. Not just wrong, but physically impossible. It doesn't matter how well the character development is done. If the facts are wrong, the knowledgeable reader's suspension of disbelief is not just interrupted, it's shattered.

And that is so unnecessary.

So take the time to get the details right.

Ask.

And if your book involves another culture, ask people from that culture to read it and give you feedback. No matter how much research you do, nothing will take the place of feedback from people of that culture. There is a thread in my novel *Wild Bird* that involves a Southern Paiute storyteller. I knew that including it at all was a risk, but Native American storytelling and teachings are an integral part of wilderness therapy programs like the one where *Wild Bird* is set, so to authentically represent the camp, they needed to be part of the story.

But I was acutely aware of how much I had to learn, so in order to respectfully include a culture that was not my own, I had to make sure I got the Paiute thread right.

Like, really, really right.

I did everything I could research-wise to accomplish this.

And when I was pretty confident that I'd done a good job, we reached out to some members of the Southern Paiute Nation for feedback on the manuscript, and after getting notes, I went back to my story and made adjustments.

You can't wing it. You can't pull characters from other cultures or occupations out of "central casting." Devote whatever time it takes. It can put the actual writing on hold for days or weeks or longer. However long it takes, get it right.

Once you begin researching a subject, you may discover you have trouble stopping. The world is full of such interesting things! Like, did you know there really are six-horned goats that climb trees? Dave Sanchez discovers them in *The Gecko & Sticky,* and you would think they're made up, but they're not. How could you *not* spend half the day reading about them?

Which is the reason I wind up with research binders that are sometimes thicker than the final manuscript. The world is full of such interesting things! But just as too little research can ruin a story, so can too much. Once you've spent time immersed in discovery, it's really tempting to insert what you've learned—to wedge it in somewhere so it doesn't go to waste—but don't do that, either! A novel is not a how-to manual or a dumping ground for information. It's a story. If your research contributes to the believability of the story or adds to its texture, use it. Once your reader senses that they're being "educated," you've gone too far.

Finding the balance takes finessing, but you owe it to your story, you owe it to the people and situations you're representing, and you owe it to your readers to get it right.

# · IV ·

# SPECIAL CASES

# 29

# MYSTERIES

The first time a kid told me "I don't like mysteries," I was like *Wait. Whoa. No. You can't mean that. How can you not like mysteries?*

But the truth is, one bad mystery *can* spoil the whole bunch, girl.

All books, but mysteries especially, are like apples. If you bite into a good one—it's crisp and juicy and sweet, with just a little tartness—you'll go back for another. But if it's mushy or mealy or leaves a sour taste in your mouth, you'll probably start choosing different kinds of fruit.

Likewise with mysteries. Bite into a bad one and there goes the whole genre. But start with one that's crisply plotted, with juicy twists and turns, and the reader will be in search of delicious seconds. And thirds. And soon they'll become a mystery buff.

By mystery, I'm referring to the classic whodunit, where the culprit is unknown and the reader, alongside the detective, tries to puzzle out who has committed the crime.

So what makes a good mystery?

I think it's easier to define what makes a bad one. In my analysis, there are three types that make people turn away from the genre.

First, there's the sort where on page, say, six, your mystery-solving radar goes up and you think, *Hmm, I bet So-and-So's the culprit.* Two or three hundred pages later, it turns out that, yeah, So-and-So *was* the culprit. When that happens, the reader feels robbed. Why'd they waste all that time reading to find out whodunit when they had it figured out on page six?

What makes a book like this less irritating is when the characters are worth spending those extra couple hundred pages with. Maybe they're funny. Or their sarcastic wit works for you. Maybe you just enjoyed hanging out with that particular gumshoe.

But some mystery writers care more about clever twists and turns than about character. And often, most notably in kids' books, the mystery protagonist can come across as being overly clever, annoyingly and unrealistically smart, and not at all someone you'd enjoy spending time with in real life.

Read one of those and, yeah, you'll be convinced that mysteries are not for you.

The second type of mystery that results in an unsatisfying experience is when the author "discovers whodunit along with the protagonist."

I've heard more than a few authors describe their process this way.

Well, hello? That is totally unfair to the reader. You're selling them mushy apples! If you as the author don't know who the bad guy is, how can you plant clues? How can you structure a twisted yet directional plot? How can you guide us through the story when *you don't know where you're going*?

Don't get me started on mushy mysteries.

*Ptooey.*

The final kind of whodunit that turns people off is when the author cheats. They kill off people, lead you to red herrings galore, twist you and turn you and keep you flipping the pages while you feverishly shuffle a short list of suspects in your mind, and then, *voilà,* they reveal the culprit along with some hocus-pocus of information or the sudden reappearance of a character they'd killed off earlier (without giving even a *hint* that they might still be alive).

That's not clever. That's not exciting. That's not—*whoosh*—a Big Reveal.

That's cheating.

If you're interested in writing whodunits, commit to fair play. And adopt the philosophy that mystery writing is not a showcase for how clever *you* are, but is, instead, an opportunity to show how clever you can make your *reader* feel.

This is accomplished by planting subtle clues and red herrings throughout the book and in such a way that the reader solves the mystery at about the same time—ideally slightly *before*—the gumshoe does.

This "slightly before" advice may run contrary to a desire to elicit gasps with your Big Reveal, but if your reader comes away feeling clever and satisfied and flush with enthusiasm for the book, you win. They will seek out another book by you because they enjoyed themselves. *They* felt smart. If they come away feeling cheated or robbed, *ptooey*, you lose.

While I'm on the subject, let me point out something for the adult-mystery-writing world. Youth mystery writers do not "just write for kids." We build your audience. We build mystery lovers who will pursue that love as adults by seeking out adult mysteries.

Love developed in youth can last a lifetime.

So if you're a mystery lover, discover good ones you can hand to kids.

And if you want to be a mystery writer at any level, remember: No mushy apples.

No rotten cores.

Let your reader take a nice, juicy bite out of crime by plotting carefully and playing fairly.

# 30

## A SERIES IS BORN

I was in the throes of teaching an algebra class how to factor trinomials when the wall phone in my classroom started ringing. Being in the middle of a lesson, I let the call roll over to voice mail.

A short while later, the office secretary buzzed my room. "Wendelin?"

"Yes?"

"You need to pick up the phone."

Panic engulfed me. This felt like when I'd learned about my brother's death the year before.

"Who is it?" I asked.

"Something about New York? They say it's important. Pick up the phone."

Mostly I was relieved that it couldn't be anything to do with another family tragedy. None of us were in New York.

So I picked up the phone.

And I learned that my editor—who had recently moved to a different publishing house—was offering to buy all four of the Sammys at once, with an option for more.

I tried to be cool and collected on the phone, but how long had I waited for this moment? How many *years?*

So the minute I hung up, I did what any sensible teacher would do—I jumped up on my desk and yelled, "Yabba dabba doo!"

And all the students in my class did what any sensible kids would do—they looked at me with squinty eyes and said, "What is *wrong* with you?"

With that phone call, a series was born. And I didn't really think about it at the time, but there was no guarantee that the series would be successful, or that Sammy's adventures would continue past the fourth installment, let alone all the way to eighteen.

I've become increasingly aware of how fortunate I am to have been able to reach the end of the Sammy Keyes story arc, to have gotten to the last book as envisioned, to have had the heart-wrenching honor of typing the last line—something that still chokes me up to think about.

Not all series writers get that.

Out in the general population there's an assumption that an author can continue writing books in a series for as long as they'd like. It doesn't work that way. Factored into the continuation of the series are sales figures. If the books don't earn their keep, the publisher will cut off future additions to the series, sometimes without warning.

So eighteen novels published across sixteen years is an anomaly, especially in present-day publishing.

Several factors contributed to my successfully reaching the end of Sammy's story, not the least of which was having the same editor for all eighteen books. Editors tend to change publishing houses, and once yours is gone, so is the primary champion of your series. Despite assurances or intentions, things can quickly take a dead-end turn if your editor leaves.

So through sixteen years of changes in-house, through paradigm shifts in publishing and strong winds blowing hard from differing directions, my editor steadied Sammy's ship, kept sounding her horn, and managed to get us safely to port.

If she had jumped ship, I'm pretty sure we wouldn't have made it.

But back to the beginning, when we'd just set sail.

Winning the Edgar for *Sammy Keyes and the Hotel Thief* helped get Sammy noticed. And it was beneficial for the series' launch because the first three Sammys (*Hotel Thief, Skeleton Man,* and *Sisters of Mercy*) were all available when the award was announced. My editor buying the first four Sammys at once was part of the publisher's plan to release the books at about six-month intervals to "quickly establish it as a series." So if someone read and loved the new "best children's mystery of the year," they could jump on the next title, and the next.

And so we were off, propelled by a little luck, some good planning, and the reward of optimism persistently applied that allowed for multiple books to be waiting in the wings.

Still, all this did not guarantee it would be smooth sailing ahead. Future books were signed up two at a time, with no guarantee that there'd be an offer on the next two.

So how do you keep wind in a series' sails? How do you keep readers interested and hungry for the next installment, wishing for more, rather than thinking you've lost your touch and should have quit writing the series a long time ago?

As you now know, I became a series writer kind of by accident. So it wasn't until I'd begun the fifth book that I really looked out at the horizon and took in the vast expanse between where I was and where I wanted to go. If each book took place about a month later in Sammy's life, and if my mission was to get Sammy through middle school safely, then I had my work cut out for me.

It was all too new and exciting to recognize then, but losing steam or burning out was a real possibility for me.

Fortunately, I stumbled onto a way to avoid it by employing another old adage: *Absence makes the heart grow fonder.* Obviously, I adore Sammy Keyes. But what kept me excited to continue writing about her was, in part, spending time away from her.

I didn't accomplish this by "taking a break" and not writing. You know my brain by now—I would have run right back to her!

Instead, I accomplished this by writing stand-alone novels between Sammy Keyes installments.

After the sixth Sammy Keyes title, I wrote *Flipped,* then went back to Sammy. After the eighth, I wrote *Swear to Howdy,* then went back to Sammy. With my sons becoming readers,

I was inspired to write the Shredderman books for younger kids, then went back to Sammy. And every time I returned to Sammy World, it was like coming home. It was a reunion with my favorite girl and the expanding cast of quirky characters. We got to reminisce a little about the past, but more important, we got to discover the future.

Because Sammy was growing and her situation was evolving, writing the next installment never felt stale or even routine. And because I had enough time to start to *miss* her while I spent time with characters in other books, I never felt stagnation or boredom set in. It was always exciting to come back, and when an author feels that for a project, the reader can feel it in the story. So if you're thinking about writing a series, here's the hit list of what I'd recommend:

1. *Create a character you love.* And make sure he or she is one you can love over the long haul. Give them flaws and room to grow. If your characters have no room to grow, they will stagnate, and so will your writing.

2. *Have a story arc to your series.* Without change, you will get bored-bored-bored and your once-joyful creative outlet will become a deadline-driven job. (And don't think readers can't tell when that happens.)

3. *Do not become chained to your series.* Go away and come back refreshed.

4. *Have a goal for your characters.* This applies to *each*

book, and also to the whole series. With every installment, have something new to say, and with the series, have an end goal in mind. Sammy Keyes books are about more than the mystery. Each title explores a different theme or moral dilemma. So while the mystery is intriguing and suspenseful and fun to write, the theme is what gave me new ideas to explore.

Bottom line: When writing a genre series (mystery, sci-fi, romance, etc.), don't expect the genre to do the heavy lifting for you. Always have some bigger idea to convey. That way, each book feels fresh, rather than like something you've retooled from an earlier installment.

And while I'm on the subject, let me just add that retooling is the death knell of series writing. You know what I'm talking about. You've started reading a series and love-love-love it, then as you move along through the titles, the stories begin to lose their zing. Characters are described using phrases you've read in earlier installments or can repeat by heart. The stories seem formulaic and the author seems uninspired. If *they* don't love it anymore, why should you? Oh, you'll go along for a few books, hoping the author will snap out of it and recapture the magic they displayed earlier in the series, but finally you give up. You break up. You're done.

Being a reader who'd had this experience on more than a few occasions, I didn't want to be a writer who repeated it. Instead, I found myself trying to *raise* the bar with each new

Sammy Keyes title. I never wanted to hear people say, *Eh. Been there, done that.* So when I read reviews that said things like *How can these books keep getting better and better?* not just the writer in me, but the *reader* in me was elated.

Adopting the attitude of continued improvement was definitely a factor in my making it to the end of the series. I respected my readers' investment in the world I'd created, and they, in turn, stuck with me to the end.

So if you're thinking about writing a series, commit to conscious and conscientious quality and development. Do not take your readers for granted. If you find yourself feeling burdened or bored as the writer, take a break. If that doesn't work, wrap it up and get out.

You—and everyone else—will be glad you did.

# 31

# WORLD-BUILDING

I've shared with you the unexpected benefit of not having the first Sammys picked up for publication until there were four of them. Looking back, it was really a gift to be able to reexamine the beginning and restructure, reinforce, and revamp.

However, during that process I failed to notice one big mistake.

So did my husband.

And my editor.

And the copy editor and proofreaders.

And yet, well after publication, I realized there was a crucial error that any middle schooler would recognize, one I couldn't simply correct in future printings. It permeated *everything*.

*Sammy Keyes and the Hotel Thief* takes place during the first week of Sammy's seventh-grade year, in September.

Sammy is thirteen and makes a big deal about that fact in that book.

Also in *Hotel Thief*, Sammy confirms to Madame Nashira (the fortune-teller living at the Heavenly Hotel) that she is an Aries, which puts Sammy's birthday somewhere between March twenty-first and April nineteenth.

Which means that Sammy would be turning fourteen in seventh grade.

Which means she got held back, she started school late, or . . . I goofed.

And yes, I goofed.

This actually didn't occur to me until I started getting fan mail from people wanting to know what Sammy's birth date was. Like, what exact day.

When I was writing that scene with Madame Nashira, I chose a zodiac sign that matched Sammy's personality. It was the first—and I thought only—book. I didn't think it mattered.

But to Sammy fans—now known as Sammiacs—it did.

Like, *a lot.*

Those letters started after the sixth book (*Hollywood Mummy*), which, in Sammy World, takes place in February and has a focus on Sammy's mother's age (and how Lana's fudged it so much in order to land a starring role that she would be too young to be Sammy's mother).

The mistake sat devilishly on my shoulder as I wrote the seventh book (*Search for Snake Eyes*), which takes place in March. What kept blocking a solution was that Sammy was smart and observant and did okay in school. And she'd been in the same town since before she'd started kindergarten and had never been homeschooled. It didn't make sense that she'd been held back. And yet her age said plainly that she *had*, and I was running out of time. Her birthday was looming, just one book away.

What was I going to do?

I considered ignoring her birthday altogether. Each title takes place over the span of about a week in Sammy's life. That span didn't *have* to include her birthday, right? I could just not mention it. But . . . then what? Never mention her age again?

Just like I do with a mystery that isn't fairly plotted, I get annoyed when I read books with obvious patches. The explanation dump that accompanies the author's need for a new character, or some unrevealed-until-now talent, or coincidental knowledge, or a convenient past experience . . . it always feels like a bad Bondo job to me.

And I didn't want an ugly patch in Sammy World.

Ugh to Bondo!

But . . . where was the solution? Everything I thought of felt like a cover-up. How could I have made such a stupid mistake?

On a flight home from New York after my second "dress to kill" Edgar Awards banquet, where *Sammy Keyes and the Curse of Moustache Mary* was one of five nominees, I resumed agonizing over the fact that it was time to start the "April" book and I still didn't know what I was going to do about the age issue. It had been a great few days in New York celebrating Sammy, but it was marred by knowing that I was harboring this terrible secret.

It was a five-hour flight, I had a window seat, I was pretty exhausted, and it would have been easy to close my eyes and tell myself I'd figure it out later.

But instead, I closed my eyes and forced my mind onto the issue. Every time it wandered off, I brought it back. And swirling around inside the batter of my mushy thoughts were Lana and her single-mother situation, her desire to be a star, and her lying about her age.

She kept popping up. Like a lump in the batter that wouldn't smooth out.

Deceptive, self-absorbed, secretive Lana.

Half the flight later I was nodding off when, *ding*, it happened. As we were cruising at thirty-five thousand feet above the earth, my mental oven popped open and there it was, the most beautiful, fully baked, *brilliant* solution.

Bondo wasn't even in the same universe as this solution!

I gasped.

I literally held my cheeks.

And then I dove into my bag, pulled out a notebook, and started scribbling. By the time I landed in Los Angeles, I had *Sammy Keyes and the Psycho Kitty Queen* sketched out and was dying to get going on it.

This idea—this solution—made it look like I had *planned* the age mistake. It made complete sense with the characters' personalities and with the events up to that point and opened up a whole new story line for the series that would work great moving forward. No spoilers, but instead a useful nugget for any writer: Learn to explore the moral *failings* of your characters for plot devices and behavior motivators—it will open up new and interesting paths for you.

I told myself that I would never spill the truth about having made the mistake, but here I've gone and told you, not just to advise you to look at things from a different angle, but also to warn you to be careful. Whatever you put into your first book, you will live with for the rest of the series.

And also to stress that if you're fortunate enough to gain an audience for a series of books, be aware that your readers may want to know things about the world you've built—things you have not yet considered. This is a huge compliment. It means they're thinking about your world outside the story line you've presented. It means they care.

Fans like that *will* find your mistakes, and when they do, they will not gleefully exclaim, *Aha, I caught a mistake!* Their suspended disbelief will come crashing down around them and they will be really disappointed—even upset—to think that they care more than you do.

Bottom line: Series-building—world-building—is an honor not to be taken lightly. And in the event you do make a mistake, respect your readers by avoiding a sloppy patch. There is always a solution out there. Even if you have to go to thirty-five thousand feet to find it!

# 32

## CHAPTER BOOKS

When my sons were becoming independent readers, I was re-introduced to early chapter books. We'd spent lots of time with picture books, but the step up to books that were more text-heavy, with only the occasional black-and-white illustration, was a big one.

I found that my sons had limited patience. Without illustrations to hold their interest, they would be upside down and backward on the couch, going, "But, Mom, it's so boring!"

"No, it's not," I would assure them. "Just sit here and give it a chance."

That was a tough sell. Once they'd decided that a book was boring, there was no convincing them otherwise. So back to the library I'd go, bringing home stacks of books, hoping I'd found some that spoke to my kids.

Through this process, I started analyzing what worked for them and what didn't. And it sent me back to remembering what had worked for *me* at that age and what hadn't. When I was a kid, I "read to the illustration." I wanted to know what it was about. I would tell myself to get to the picture, *then* take a break. Of course, often I'd keep going, but usually I'd read *to* something—the illustration, the end of a chapter, a break in the chapter . . . some marker that seemed like a good place to rest.

My boys also helped me remember what made me want to *stop* reading when I was a kid. Besides the author taking too long to get into a story—long, descriptive paragraphs being the prime offender—the biggest culprit was coming upon a dense double-page spread of text.

Too many words.

It wasn't just the two unillustrated pages of text; it was the density of that text. If what faced me was a wall of words, I got tired just looking at it and would want to stop. But if the pages had short, punchy paragraphs or back-and-forth dialogue, I could make it through and keep going.

I didn't look at it this way at the time, but it was the *white space* on the page that made me a stronger reader. It gave me the motivation to keep going, and made me feel proud of myself when I turned the next page.

My sons inspired my Shredderman books, and when I began writing them, it was with a keen eye on creating stories that my kids and their friends would like.

White space—check!

Lots of action—check!

Kid humor—check!

Enough exclamation points to drive the literati crazy—check and double-check!!!

Shredderman is the cyber-superhero alter ego of Nolan Byrd, a fifth-grade boy who power-walks, forgets that his socks are supposed to go *inside* his pant legs, and loves to nerd out on computers and science. He is also the favorite target of a big hulking bully named Bubba Bixby.

Being around lots of kids Nolan's age and having a son who was a science nerd with very little interest in ordinary tasks (like making sure his socks went on the proper side of his pant legs) got me into the groove of the character, and the project turned into a "quartet" of illustrated books. Each book is slightly longer than the previous one (to build those "reading muscles"). Shredderman's influence expands with each title, spreading from Nolan's school, to his town, to the country, and finally to the world.

The books—and their antibullying message—were really well received, and the premise of a nerdy kid taking down a brawny bully by using his brains and a secret website he builds was enthusiastically embraced by critics and teachers.

Time went by, and the internet—and how people use it—changed. Suddenly the bullies online were worse than the ones on the playground. And I started getting asked, *How is what Nolan does any different from what Bubba does?*

Online bullying *is* an awful problem. And even though Nolan's purpose for having his website is to do good—which includes getting Bubba to stop being mean to kids at school—and even though his site is a defense against an ongoing bullying problem, we *don't* want to give kids the wrong idea regarding internet use.

Here's where having an underlying theme and an overarching story line to your series can save you. Because the Shredderman quartet isn't just about stopping the bully.

It's about redemption.

That doesn't come into clear focus until book four (*Enemy Spy*), but when it does, concerns vanish. And the fact that the tech (and illustrations of it) is now outdated (e.g., bulky computer monitors) doesn't matter either. Because the stories themselves appeal to kids, and the themes of finding the superhero inside you and standing up for yourself override them. And that the series is wrapped in the unifying theme of redemption helps it hold up over time.

What will stay constant is the need to match budding readers with their interests and reading ability. So if you're considering writing chapter books, make sure your vocabulary is appropriate, the sentence length and structure are accessible, and the design—including white space—appeals to kids.

Then try out chapters on your intended audience. Pay attention to them. Are they engaged? Excited? Asking for more? If so, great. If not, listen to what they tell you. Pinpoint the place or the reason you lost them, and revise accordingly.

# 33

---

# SEQUELS

If you're fortunate enough to find yourself in a position where you're being asked for a sequel to a book you've written, congratulations. And conventional wisdom says, *Do it!*

It's also just nice to have readers who are invested enough in your story to want a follow-up. I cannot even begin to count the number of times I've been asked for a sequel to *Flipped*. Who'd have guessed that a "small story" would grow to have such a large impact and become a feature film?

Not me.

The requests for a *Flipped* sequel have come from both kids and adults, and although some are downright demanding, most are very polite. And passionate. Pages and pages of passionate. Elaborate-suggestions-for-sequel-plots passionate. Begging-to-name-Bryce-and-Juli's-future-babies passionate. Promising-me-their-kingdom (or at least their collection of Pez dispensers) passionate.

The Pez offer was tempting. (There were pictures.) And the truth is, it would make great financial sense to write a sequel to *Flipped*.

Yet, I have held out.

This is not because I have a limited imagination or wouldn't like the money. And it's not because I don't have a story in mind of what happens to Bryce and Juli. I do.

It's because I think it's the wrong thing to do.

With *Flipped*, I wanted to achieve a delicate balance of realistic and idealistic. And I like that the ending is an awakening. A sunrise. What's ahead is up to Bryce and Juli, and we trust them now to make good choices.

My hope was that the reader would close the cover and collect their thoughts. I wanted the story to linger in their mind, to settle in and help them reflect on their own relationships. Writing a sequel would obfuscate that purpose; it would spoon-feed an answer about the characters' future, when what's important is how the story impacts the *reader's* future.

*What path do you want to take?*

*What kind of people do you want at your side?*

*Are you ready to find the courage to be true to yourself?*

Since for many of my readers applying these questions to their own life *has* been the impact of reading *Flipped*, I believe I'm making the right choice by not extending the story.

Because sometimes a sequel subtracts.

Even if the sequel is a great story, well executed, the net result can be less than the sum of the parts.

There is no rule about sequels, and there are myriad reasons to write them (or not). So my best advice if you do find yourself in such a fortunate position is simply to remain clear on the *purpose* of your work and let that purpose guide you.

· V ·

# SEEDS AND SPROUTS

## 34

# ORIGIN STORIES

The most common question I get asked is *Where did you get the idea for that book?* I used to assume that the person asking wanted to know generally how I develop ideas for the stories I write. You know, little tips and tricks to stimulate the imagination.

But after I've given my best advice, the questioner usually persists. What they really want to know is how I got the idea for a particular, specific book.

Which, no matter how often it happens, is always a little surprising to me. Maybe that's because I *don't* really want to know too much about an author's personal thread in the story. It messes with the picture I've painted in my mind. It makes it so I can't shake off the author's presence, and the whole idea (in my opinion) of fictional work is that the reader becomes so absorbed in the story that they forget there's an author at all.

Also, an idea is *not* the story. An idea is the *seed* of a story, and I believe writers should be seed collectors. Not only should you gather ideas, but you should give them a chance to germinate in the fertile soil of your mind.

Give. Them. Time.

The hardy ones—the sustainable ones—will eventually push to the surface. When they do, warm them in the sunshine of your focus, care, and love, and they *will* bloom.

Still, I find that people are really fascinated by a novel's origin story. So what follows is a handful of those—ones selected to illustrate how ideas were planted in me, and how those ideas grew into stories. I hope you enjoy them, and I hope they will help you find new ways to recognize and nurture seeds of your own.

# 35

# BOY SCOUT VS. HOODLUM

Structure is not story. The idea of two sides to a story—boy's side, girl's side—is a mechanical device. The *story* is something completely different, and in the case of *Flipped*, it's one about two kids learning to see each other for who they really are (instead of what they look like).

It's a story I wish I'd read when I was a kid.

Or a teen.

Or, shoot, an adult.

As it was, it took me way too long to learn how to look beneath the surface of people. Especially guys. Like my friends, I would fall for the gorgeous ones.

I will drop you now inside my Dark Era, take you back in time to my early twenties, when the Bad Stuff had happened and life seemed to be all about survival and digging a way out of the Pit of Despair. My family—Mom and "the kids"—were a tightly knit bunch then as we struggled to rise out of the literal ashes of an arsonist's destruction of my parents' factory while also grieving Dad's death. We worked long, hard days that folded into weeks and stretched into years, but a sense of purpose kept us going.

During the Dark Era, I learned a lot of skills. By necessity, I became a carpenter, a plumber, an electrician, a roofer, a drywaller, a janitor, an accountant, and a heavy-equipment operator—and if you've ever read in one of my book bios that I was a forklift driver, this was the era of that.

When we'd finally reached a point where we could hire people to help us, we weren't very good at holding on to employees. And no wonder. The pay was lousy and the work was often labor-intensive. And there was the unspoken expectation that hired hands should be willing to work as hard as we did.

We didn't really understand how strange the dynamic was to outsiders. We were focused on the work, not on the fact that we were too young to be tackling this enterprise. I look back and see so many flaws in our reasoning and approach, but at the time it was all about helping our mother and doing what we could to not have our father's life and legacy end on such a tragic note. We were worker ants, willing to get up early, pull on our boots and coveralls, hit the job hard, and keep at it for as long as it took, even if that meant sleeping on cots at the business and working weekends.

What hired hand could live up to that?

So employees came and they went; some were good and deserved better, others were just out of their element. And over time it became clear that we needed a different way to screen potential hires. Competency in basic math was important for the job, so the future teacher in me came up with the idea to have applicants complete the standard paperwork and also take a relevant math test. I constructed one, and while I was at it, I came up with a second test that had diagrams of equipment they'd be using with attendant questions asking fundamental things like which valves should be opened or closed to effect a specified change, or what a certain gauge indicated. You didn't really have to know anything about the equipment; it was just applied logic.

When the applicants turned in their paperwork, I jotted down little notes based on my initial impression of them. Nothing elaborate. Just one or two words like *polite, salesy, shifty* . . . that sort of thing. And at the end of a very long day, I reviewed all the applications and graded the papers.

The results were dismal. Scores were shockingly low on both tests, but the equipment diagram test was a disaster. There was only one applicant who had done well—*really* well, in fact. The trouble was the notation I'd jotted down about him.

*Hoodlum.*

I didn't have to try to remember which applicant this was. I knew immediately. Long scruffy hair, full beard, tattered Levi's jacket . . . and he smelled like cigarettes. I'd actually been anxious for him to leave. To me, he was scary. Almost menacing.

The next-closest scores belonged to an applicant whose notation was *Boy Scout*. I remembered exactly who he was too, and in our family of Scouts, that description meant only good things.

But his second-best scores didn't compare to the Hoodlum's.

My brother had seen the Hoodlum drive off in an old primer-gray truck—loud, wide wheels, lots of junk on the dash, rock music blaring from the stereo. When I told him about the Hoodlum's nearly perfect score, he said, "There's no way we're hiring that guy."

Enter the sibling dynamic. After a little back-and-forth about it, I started digging in, convincing myself that we *should* hire the Hoodlum. After all, what were we judging here? He'd scored great on the tests!

The ensuing argument went something like this:

Him: Forget it. We're hiring the Boy Scout.

Me: No, we're hiring the Hoodlum.

Boy Scout!

Hoodlum!

Boy Scout!

Hoodlum!

Boy Scout!

Hoodlum!

Eventually, as we always had before, we reached a compromise: We would hire both applicants. My brother would train the Boy Scout, and I would train the Hoodlum.

Fine!

Fine!

We'll see who lasts longer!

Yeah, we'll see!

I made the call while I was still fired up and began worrying about it immediately after hanging up. Hadn't I been anxious for the guy to leave? Didn't I think he was scary?

What had I gotten myself into?

I'd asked the Hoodlum if he could start the next day—a Saturday. He'd said yes, but I'd heard the reluctance in his voice.

So maybe he wouldn't show up. Maybe I'd admit to my brother that, yeah, I'd been dumb and move on.

But Saturday morning, the Hoodlum appeared. Early, even. So I issued him his boots and coveralls and showed him around, and before long we were on task, doing a pretty mundane, repetitive job.

And that's when the questions started. And they never seemed to stop. As one workday bled into the next, he kept asking me seemingly random stuff. What did I think of this, what did I think of that, what was my favorite book, band, movie. . . . He was not chatting me up. He just liked to talk. Actually, no. It was more than that. He liked to *debate,* and there was no getting away from it.

It wasn't the questions that bothered me, but the inevitable follow-up questions. Like *Is it your favorite song because of lyrical content or chord progression?*

WHY CAN'T IT JUST BE MY FAVORITE SONG?

And then one day there was this: "Do you believe in ethical absolutes?"

Ethical absolutes? What the bleep?

I'm pretty sure I was kinda testy when I asked him to explain.

"You know," he said, "when something's always right, or always wrong?"

"For example . . . ?"

"Like . . . say . . . is it ever okay to murder someone?"

This from the Hoodlum.

WHY DIDN'T I DO A BACKGROUND CHECK?

I wasn't very good at answering these questions. I hadn't spent a lot of time thinking philosophical thoughts over the last few years. I'd made to-do lists. Long, practical to-do lists. Ones that would roll over to the next day, and the next. Bottomless to-do lists that left me too exhausted to spend time mind-jockeying over things like ethical absolutes, or whether I liked a song because of its chord progression or its lyrical content, or what the rational principles for establishing universal values of right and wrong should be.

I had work to do!

But after work, the questions lingered. And it bugged me that I didn't have answers. *Were* there ethical absolutes? *Was* it ever okay to murder someone?

At the time, I was in a relationship with a guy we'll call the Dashing Man. He was the classic tall-dark-and-handsome variety, and really, he looked like he should be running around in a white puffy shirt with a fencing sword in hand. I had fallen hard.

During dinners out with the Dashing Man, I would ask him questions posed to me by the Hoodlum. I wanted to discuss them so I could go back to work with ammunition. Well-crafted answers!

So I asked, "Do you think there's such a thing as an ethical absolute?"

The Dashing Man gave me a dashing squint. "An ethical absolute? What's that?"

"You know, like, say, is it ever okay to murder someone?"

"To *murder* someone?" Deeper squint, not at all dashing. "Wendelin, what's gotten into you?"

Clearly, the Dashing Man was not helping me stockpile ammunition. As a matter of fact, my questions began to annoy him. Why couldn't his favorite song just be his favorite song? Why did I want to analyze everything? Why was I asking all these questions?

Which only created more questions inside me.

Questions that were starting to change the way I saw . . . everything.

So, to make a very long, very convoluted story short, the Boy Scout turned in his boots and coveralls after about a month.

And I married the Hoodlum.

# 36

# FLIPPED

So. What's the Hoodlum story got to do with *Flipped,* a book about a girl who raises chickens in her backyard and likes to climb trees? What's it got to do with a boy who hates that annoying girl and avoids her at all costs?

The seed idea of learning to see past a person's surface was planted with the Hoodlum experience, but it stayed dormant for years, until it was watered by new experiences.

As a teacher, I saw teens doing the same thing I had done—crushing on someone because they were cute or gorgeous or hot or whatever. Girls did it, boys did it, and usually very little attention was paid to whether there was substance to back up those strong emotions.

Turns out, it's a pretty universal thing. Almost certainly instinctive. But more is required for sustainable relationships than biological drive. For those, you have to learn to dig a little deeper.

In addition to teaching six classes each day, I ran the computer club, the chess club, the school newspaper, and the year-book. So I really didn't have time to be anywhere but in my room during the school day, and there were always students hanging around at break, at lunch, and after school. They ate their lunches, played chess, caught up on homework, or found a quiet corner to shed some tears.

Their constant presence was how I learned that kids can be really good at giving each other really bad advice. They mean well. They're trying. But wow. *Cringe.* No. Please.

And of course my attempts at sharing hard-won wisdom regarding romance fell on deaf ears. They knew I meant well. They could see I was trying. But I was a teacher.

Wow. *Cringe.* No. Please.

But still. If only I could really talk to them.

If only they would really listen.

But how, when they were in a place where they only wanted to listen to each other?

And *this* was when the seed popped through the surface.

Why not let my characters do the talking?

The idea of two characters learning to really see each other "in the proper light" grew fast and strong. The sycamore tree, the chickens, the Basket Boys, the everything-else were off-shoots that sprang from a seed that had been germinating for years.

It was springtime for *Flipped.*

It burst out and became its own living, growing, blossoming thing.

Not a hoodlum in sight.

# 37

# BREAKFAST IN BIRMINGHAM

Another seed was planted at an event in Birmingham, Alabama—a breakfast hosted by my publisher. It took a series of forever flights to get there, and I arrived at my hotel room late and exhausted. I called home to check in. The kids, then six and eight years old, were not happy. I could tell from my husband's voice that he, too, had had a long day.

"Remind me why you're doing this?" he asked.

The truth is, I wasn't really sure. My in-house publicist had arranged things. It was part of some national English teacher conference. Who knew there was such a thing? And why hold it so late in November? Regardless, in a moment filled with optimistic energy, I'd committed to going.

That energy had abandoned me when a delayed flight had messed with my connection. And now, in my travel-weary state, all I knew was that I had to get to bed. Breakfast was early and

I was booked on an afternoon flight back home the next day. I didn't even bother to unpack.

At breakfast, I sat at a round table with a handful of librarians in a moderate-sized room that held perhaps twenty such tables. I remember the publisher introducing all the authors present and saying a few words about each writer's most recent contribution to children's literature. I remember he ended his remarks about Sammy Keyes with "Long may she wave," which I thought was awesome.

But really, that's pretty much all I remember about the breakfast.

What I remember about *afterward* was being dropped off at the airport, stressing to get through security on time, and then finding myself crammed up against a window in sardine class with a couple and their unhappy almost-two-year-old, the three of them more than filling the middle and aisle seats.

I called my husband before takeoff. Between juggling work and child care, it had been a long twenty-four hours for him, too. "So you're telling me you flew to Birmingham for breakfast," he said, summing up my summary.

"Looks like," I said.

The almost-two-year-old grabbed and yanked my hair. I cowered farther against the window and whimpered.

Add sticky hair to the trip's delights.

"You okay?" my husband asked as the kid squalled and lunged again.

Like I could explain? "I'm really looking forward to being home."

A moment of silence from him and then, "Promise me you'll never go to Birmingham for breakfast again."

That was a no-brainer. "I promise."

The trip immediately worked its way into our family lexicon. "Is this another breakfast in Birmingham?" became code for assessing whether a trip was worth taking. Because from all indicators, breakfast in Birmingham had not been.

But about a year after the breakfast, a completely unexpected thing happened: A school district in Alabama wanted to hire me for an extended stay so I could visit all their middle schools. The head librarian had been at the breakfast and had, apparently, taken a shine to me.

So I returned to Alabama, and this time I unpacked. This time I learned firsthand what "Southern hospitality" is all about. Everyplace I went, people fussed over me, making sure I was doing okay and had enough to eat, making sure the students were respectful and attentive. I had never been *ma'am*'d before in my life, but now every single sentence directed my way ended in *ma'am*. Even the school lunches were different from anything I'd experienced, and I came to discover the secret ingredient that made my most-loathed-as-a-child vegetable, lima beans, delicious.

Bacon.

I even went up for seconds.

So I had a wonderful time in Alabama, but the thing I loved

most was listening to the language that surrounded me like an ethereal chuckle—the colorful expressions that floated past me. *Dumber'n a mud fence. Madder'n a wet hen. Makes my teeth itch. Poor as pig tracks* . . . I was the California-raised daughter of Dutch immigrants. It was all new to me.

On my very last day, while I was out to lunch with all the librarians and the superintendent of schools, the Southern expressions were flying as the conversation turned (as it invariably does when school folk get together) to what was going on in education. "Oh, he's happy as a pig in sunshine over that" came flying one way. "I'm sick of ropin' dead cows" went the other.

Since they were busy talking among themselves, I surreptitiously began scribbling down the expressions on a paper napkin, trying to recall others I'd heard during my time there so I could share them with my husband when I got home.

And I was just starting on the back side of the napkin when I got busted.

"What y'all doing?" a librarian asked me.

I blushed, then fessed up with a guilty smile. "Writin' down the way all y'all talk?"

The group near me leaned in. "What y'all got so far?"

I read them my list, and when I was done, they said, "Well, shoot. We can do better'n that!" and proceeded to shower me with expressions. Even the superintendent chimed in.

So breakfast in Birmingham wasn't a hard paddle up a dry river for nothing after all. Because of it I met some wonderful people, talked to a gazillion kids about Sammy Keyes, had an enlightening cultural experience, and returned home with a scribbled list of expressions and great stories to share with my husband.

Breakfast had a dessert course, how nice!

And that, I thought, was the end of that.

## 38

---

# SWEAR TO HOWDY

There was no thought in my mind of writing a book using Southern language or a Southern setting.

None.

I was up to my earlobes attending to books under contract and stressed by the pace. Under pressure to write the Shredderman quartet between Sammy Keyes books, I had worried aloud to my husband several times that I'd overcommitted. Even though I was now a full-time author with a six-hour writing day while my kids were in elementary school, the deadlines nipped hard at my heels. For some inexplicable reason, it felt like I had *less* time to write now that I was doing it full-time. How could that be?

The situation was a complete flip from my precontract writing days, when nobody seemed to want my work or care that I was writing at all. It was strange to look back and realize there had been a certain luxury in nobody wanting my stuff. Not that

I would trade back—I'd worked too hard to get to this point! So I checked my complaints, redoubled my efforts, and focused.

And then one night . . .

Yes, that *is* the way it always goes.

On this particular night I was losing the battle to wait up for my husband, who was working a swing shift. As I dozed off, a scene from an almost-dream went through my mind: a car careening toward a tree, kids yanking on a rope.

I snapped to, then told myself it was only a dream. Everything was okay. But as I started to drift off again, there was the car again, careening toward a tree, and kids yanking on a rope.

I stopped the scene in my mind, tried to steer it in another direction. But it seemed to have a mind, a direction, of its own, and as I drifted off again, there it was, that car, careening toward a tree, and kids yanking on a rope.

But this time there was a voice that went along with it.

A boy's voice.

One with a Southern accent.

*Joey's blood got mixed up in mine the same way mine got mixed up in his: drop by drop, pact by pact. And there's times that makes me feel good, but there's times it creeps me out. Reminds me.*

I sat up, wide awake now, and breathless. And rather than ask the boy who he was and what the devil he was doing in my head, I grabbed a pad of paper and wrote down what he was saying.

The words just flowed, and before long, out of my pen came, "I swear to howdy, if you tell a soul."

I stopped short.

*I swear to howdy.*

It was a favorite expression of a woman I had gotten to know during my extended stay in Alabama.

And this voice in my head—it could have been one of any number of the kids I'd spent time with there.

But . . . it had been at least six months since I'd visited Alabama.

Why was this boy talking to me *now*?

Let me take a moment to confirm that creative writers are all a little crazy. We do hear voices. We talk about our characters like they're real. We *feel* the story like it's actually happening. And what happens to the people who populate our books *matters* to us.

It matters a lot.

By the time my husband came home from work, my character had a name, a family, a personality, and a mischievous best friend. And I was a goner. I barely greeted my husband before shaking the pad of paper at him. "Here. Read this!"

Despite his weary-from-a-long-day state, he obliged (because he's that kind of guy). When he was done, he gave me a baffled look, flipped back through the pages, and said, "What *is* this?"

So I told him about the car and the tree and the rope and the dream. I told him about the boy in my head.

That I could *hear* him.

That he had a story to tell.

I was wide awake and trying to explain why this boy, this story, was crucial. "What got him to the point where he thought this was okay to do? How does *any* kid get there? It starts with little things and escalates. You don't see it coming and then all of a sudden it's too late!"

Okay, I'll admit—it was after midnight and I was definitely not "reading the room." And I was a little manic, already talking about my characters like they were real.

My husband returned the pad and sighed. "It's wonderful, but . . . are you sure you want to start on this? I thought you were stressed about your deadlines."

But it was too late. I was possessed. And, unfortunately for the rest of the family, I dove into the story and didn't emerge until I'd reached the end. It was short. Only 126 pages. I didn't know if a book that length was even publishable.

And it didn't matter.

Because that's how it is when you write from a place of merging passions. This wasn't just a story about two boys and the mischief they got into. This was a story about friendship and what it meant to be a true friend. This was a story about the burning rubber of wrong turns on the highway out of childhood. This was about finding the courage to take a stand, about pulling your friend back from the brink.

The voice came to me from across the country, but it spoke for every kid who'd ever longed for a best friend to share adventures with, and for every kid who'd learned the hard way that some secrets are better confessed.

I titled it *Swear to Howdy,* sent it to my new librarian friends in Alabama for their reaction, took their suggestions, and mailed the manuscript to my editor with a note that basically said, "Surprise!"

And she said . . .

"What *is* this?"

But then she read it.

And I didn't have to explain a thing.

So, as you pursue your dreams, remember this: Dishes and laundry and the mundane can wait. They will call to you and try to convince you that you don't have time for creative pursuits, but I promise you—dishes and laundry and the mundane can wait.

They may multiply as you put them off, but they can wait.

Instead, learn to listen to the voices that call from your heart.

Learn to follow the story.

Because the *story* should be the thing that cannot wait.

# 39

## STARTING LINE

And then there's the story I battled *against* writing. The one where a teen who loves to run gets in an awful accident on the way home from a track meet and winds up losing a leg.

Ugh. What an *awful* idea. I believe in books that uplift. Create hope! One about a girl who becomes an amputee in the prime of her life?

NO!

So how in the world did the idea seed itself in my brain?

After years of doing author presentations at schools and hearing librarians talk about slashed budgets and shrinking staffing, my husband and I started an initiative called Exercise the Right to Read to bring attention to this issue and to provide a funding mechanism for schools: a "reading, running marathon" that combined literacy, fitness, and community service.

To launch the program and bring awareness to the cause,

we committed to running the New York City Marathon under the Exercise the Right to Read banner.

For the record, I am not—N O T—a running fanatic. I ran track in high school, but that was the end of my competitive running. Back then I thought cross-country runners were nuts. 5K races? Who would sign up for that? I wouldn't even tackle the 800m. The 400 was hard enough!

In college I gained my "freshman fifteen" and returned to running as a way to manage my weight. Running a mile for "recreation" seemed like a huge accomplishment, but it didn't do much to counterbalance my caloric intake. And being someone who likes to eat, rather than cutting back on that, I started running longer.

Pretty soon I was up to three miles, then five. Before long, distance running had its hooks in me and I did it for reasons besides weight control. I liked that it stabilized my mood, that it made me feel happier, more optimistic, stronger both mentally and physically.

When the Dark Era hit, running became my lifeline. I would run to escape, run to conquer, run to forget, run to sort through the meaning of life . . . and eventually, I would run to write. The stories would unfold in my head and occupy me through three, five, seven, ten miles of footfalls. Whole stretches of road vanished. Sometimes I'd look around and not really remember how I got there.

But no, I was not and have never been a running fanatic. I do not live for it; I do it to help myself live better. Getting out the door is always the battle, but when I'm done—no matter how long or short the run—I'm always glad I made myself go.

So that's the shortcut version of the long and winding road that transformed me from someone who ran 400 meters max to someone who was willing to go 26.2 miles to raise funds for libraries.

My husband and I did all the training, stuck to the schedule, learned to hydrate while running, discovered which flavors of Gu were delicious (anything chocolate) and which made me want to hurl (anything berry). We did the long-run weekends, maxing out at twenty-two miles, and reveled in the "taper"— the week prior to the race where you get to take it kind of easy and even (gasp) not run.

Then we flew to New York, got our race packets, tried (unsuccessfully) to sleep, and got on a 5:00 a.m. shuttle in downtown Manhattan that bused us over to Staten Island, where we were dropped off to become part of a field of about forty thousand other insane people.

It was November, with temperatures forecast to be in the low thirties. And armed with the theoretical knowledge that thirty-two degrees is freezing and required more than our usual shorts and T-shirt, we arrived at the starting area wearing sweats. Other people—people who knew what they were doing—had down parkas, beanies, mittens, and sleeping bags.

Sleeping bags!

Why?

Because the race had a late start time—10:00 a.m.—and sensible people wanted to stay warm and finish sleeping.

Which we certainly could have used. Anxious about logistics and not able to sleep anyway, we'd arrived on the island at 6:00 a.m., which gave us a good four hours to shiver in the November cold.

After about an hour of unsuccessfully trying to settle in, I discovered a dumpster and went diving for cardboard to sit on (because I'd learned from researching *Runaway* that it really does make a good insulator). While I was rooting around, I unearthed a pair of clean-enough socks, which I snagged and converted into mittens. But still, I shivered.

By the time the race began, all the carbo-loading I'd done for three days prior, all the glycogen I'd packed into my cells, all the excitement I'd brought with me had shivered away. I was jet-lagged, hungry, and exhausted.

And in a really grumpy mood.

My husband wasn't as bad off as I was. We have the same basic frame, but he has more muscle mass, so wasn't as cold. He's also a perennial optimist and the opposite of a complainer. As we ran, he dubbed himself my "Gu boy" and monitored my energy gel and water consumption, and kept me moving ahead with his good-natured chattering.

But still. I was not "enjoying the moment." After the first six miles, the only moment I was looking forward to was the one where I crossed the finish line, and that was still hours away.

And then around Mile 10 we came upon two runners holding the ends of a rope that sagged between them like a long, sorry-looking snake.

"Who are these idiots?" I grumbled, because the rope was

blocking my path and the marathon rules had specifically stated that there were to be no leashes or dogs or baby joggers or jump ropers or limbo-ing lunatics or . . . or . . . ropes of any kind!

If you can sigh while you're running, that's exactly what my husband did. "Just go around," he said, the strain of being my Gu boy showing.

But I didn't want to go around! I knew the shortest distance between two points is a straight line! And there were no ropes allowed on the course!

I told him this through gritted teeth and he said, "Just go around, Wendelin."

I pictured my choices as the legs of a right triangle. "I don't want to take the A leg," I told him. "Or the B leg."

"What?"

"I want to stay on the hypotenuse!"

"Wendelin!" A little exasperated now. "Go around."

So fine. I went around the idiots and their stupid rope. And as exhausted and miserable as I was, I still managed to conjure up enough energy to throw the rope guys a dirty look.

And that's when I realized that one of the runners was . . . *blind?*

This took a minute to process.

A blind runner tethered to a sighted runner by way of a rope running a *marathon?*

How could that be? How could you navigate 26.2 miles—in a crowded field of forty thousand people, with runners cutting rudely across the roadway at every water stop to grab a paper cup of Gatorade, only to dump it on the ground half finished in front of you—if you weren't able to see?

I can't even make it across my kitchen with my eyes closed! Flabbergasted, I turned to my husband and gasped, "He's *blind*."

I got a smarty-pants look back. "So . . . who's the idiot here?"

The Amazing Rope Duo was only the beginning of my exposure to extraordinary people determined to cross that marathon's finish line. There was the Old Man in Red Socks. Weathered skin over bones, he looked ninety to me. Ninety, and slowly passing me by. I told myself to keep up, but instead he steadily put distance between us until eventually his red socks bobbed out of view.

Then there was the runner who passed me like an amped-up Quasimodo, hunched over, powering forward with a determined hobble. "How is he doing that?" I asked as I watched him go. I tried to get my structurally aligned legs to pick up the pace, but again I couldn't keep up.

We saw a lot of people—including amputees—with physical challenges that you might imagine would prevent them from running a mile, let alone a marathon, but there they were, taking those 26.2 miles one determined step at a time. It was humbling. And perspective-building. What a wimp I was, whining about jet lag and fatigue and being cold. I had nothing to complain about!

The finish line of a marathon is a place of triumph. We did

cross it, and it was definitely cause for celebration, especially since a few good friends (including my editor) showed up to cheer us over it.

But more important, I discovered that the finish line of a marathon is where you'll find the strength of the human spirit on full and glorious display. I'm not talking about watching the elite runners come in. They're only on their feet for a couple of hours.

Sheez.

Sissies.

I'm talking about the people who keep moving through their pain for six, seven, eight hours. The ones whose minds won't be ruled by what ails their bodies.

The finish line of a marathon is the starting line for believing you can conquer anything.

Which is the sort of revelation that takes root in your heart and demands to grow.

# 40

## THE RUNNING DREAM

It happened on the flight home from New York. I was nodding off, little scenes from the marathon adventure ping-ponging around in my head, when I first got the idea for *The Running Dream*.

And like I said, I hated it.

This was similar to the *Swear to Howdy* experience in that I bolted awake, but at no time did voices start up in my head, and scribbling down anything related to an avid runner losing her leg was the *last* thing I wanted to do.

What I wanted was for the scene, the idea, to leave me alone.

For months, I resisted. But each time I shoved the idea away, it somehow snuck back, carrying with it a new facet, a new subtext to explore, a more focused relevance or application.

*Go away!* I told it.

But it kept sneaking back.

All the mental gnashing eventually produced audible grumblings and then verbal protestations—arguments with myself, really—to which my husband was subjected.

Eventually he said, "Why don't you just write it already?"

"Because I don't know anything about amputations or rehabilitation or prosthetic limbs!" I told him. "You can't just fake it!"

Busy on his own project, he raised an eyebrow in my direction and said, "I may know a guy."

Beware the man who "knows a guy." Besides, I didn't want to be a Snoopy Suzie, quizzing some guy about his fake leg for a story.

Cue the shudders and self-loathing.

But it turned out the guy wasn't an amputee. He was a prosthetist who had built legs for amputees. Lots of them.

*Hmm.*

I *could* see myself talking to him.

Before I contacted him, though, I did a bunch of research. Not because I was committed to writing the story, but because I am, as a rule, committed to not being disrespectful of someone else's time. Also, I hate when I'm not prepared enough to ask specific questions, or I'm still too low on the learning curve to really process a flood of new information or understand the jargon. The Scouting motto *Be Prepared* extends beyond wilderness survival—it's a good motto for interviewing people, too.

But even after all the prep work and the interview, I was still not convinced I could or should write about an amputee. The research was daunting, not to mention what it would take to capture the emotional component of going through such a trauma.

What appealed to me about the idea, however, was the universality of the premise. I thought that a *This could be me (or my best friend or my family member or . . .)* exploration of a disability would hit home in a way I'd found difficult to achieve with the teens in my classroom when it came to inclusion of kids with lifelong disabilities.

I also liked the idea of creating a teen character who could demonstrate how not to give up on a friend. When I went through the Dark Era, I really could have used a friend like that. And after I'd survived the Dark Era, I carried resentments toward people who were just . . . absent.

What I didn't recognize then is that nobody teaches you how to be a friend. You learn by example. Or experience. Many friendships happen by default—we're in the same class, on the same team, in the same neighborhood—and when one of our friends is a downer to be with or even tells us to leave them alone, well, we start looking around for new friends.

So creating an example of real friendship—of someone who would not be pushed away by the words or the actions or the attitude of her devastated friend—also had real appeal to me.

But it was still not enough.

The learning curve to write knowledgeably about an amputee was just too daunting. Also, there was nothing unique in the basic story: Someone gets knocked down and learns to get back up and live again. How often has *that* been done?

So, no.

I was not going to write this story.

Once again, I pushed it aside.

And then . . .

Yes.

And then.

This time, it was a little tickle in my brain. A question float-ing in: What would it be like for the amputee character to re-turn to school in a wheelchair and be required to sit at the back of the classroom beside a girl in a motorized wheelchair? A girl she'd walked past all year without so much as a smile or a hello.

And then . . .

How would the realization that she was now also perceived as "special needs" hit her? What would it be like to become a person others avoided eye contact with? Someone people didn't know how to engage? Someone people were uncomfortable around?

And then . . .

What would it be like to discover that the previous assump-tions she'd had about the girl in the motorized wheelchair were way off base? That the girl was, in fact, a math genius—one with a wonderful sense of humor and a kind, compassionate heart?

And with that realization . . .

What would it be like to look back at yourself and see that the whole-bodied person you used to be was less than you should have been?

That you'd been missing parts of a different kind.

And how would you move forward in the world once you'd recovered?

Would you leave the girl in the wheelchair behind?

Or would you find ways to take her with you?

And *that,* that idea, that character growth, was the linchpin. Suddenly the story, its purpose, and the theme all held together in a way that made me willing to tackle that formidable learning curve. Suddenly I wanted to know *everything.*

That "everything" turned out to take me about three years, during which I learned so much and met the most amazing people. From the young dancer who'd lost a leg to cancer, to the war vet, to the teacher whose leg had been crushed in a motorcycle accident, the many amputees I worked with to research the book all had one inspiring thing in common: They were grateful. Grateful to be alive.

Researching *The Running Dream* turned out to be one of the most rewarding experiences of my life. And because of that, I want to end this chapter with a bit of advice: Sometimes a story idea comes as a bolt out of the blue. Sometimes it creeps in over time. Sometimes it charges in and fades away. It's the ones that come in, pull up a chair, and won't leave that you should listen to.

Even if they weren't welcome, listen.

You may discover they have something important to say.

---

# 41

# MEMORY CAMP

It seems that all of my stand-alone titles are stories that come from things that have touched me on a deep emotional level. This certainly holds true for *The Secret Life of Lincoln Jones,* although this time I didn't see the story coming. I didn't know I'd been "researching" it for years. I was just trying to navigate the shifting needs of my mother as she slowly succumbed to dementia. This wasn't something to write about. It was personal. Sad. Exhausting. Private.

Far above looks or wealth or social standing, Mom valued her mind. She seemed to be most alive when she was in a feisty debate with a worthy opponent about . . . well, anything, which is why she and my husband got along so well. If she had an opportunity to wield a sword in defense of her position, she'd do so with delight.

So it was really heartbreaking to witness her mind slipping away. And although Mom was determined to remain independent, there came a point when she desperately needed help. Giving her that help was easier said than done. She became suspicious of everyone, including her own children, and was not shy about using her cane on caregivers who she thought were strangers invading her home.

When we broached alternative living situations with her, she was defiant and stubborn, and not about to leave her "cave," which was her term of endearment for the house my dad had designed and our family had built, the place we had all learned to really swing a hammer.

After a good six months of exhausting every other option, my sister and I sat her down and showed her an MRI of her brain. Mom broke into tears because she understood that the preponderance of dark spaces in the image meant that a great deal of her brain had atrophied.

"It's not your fault," we told her again and again, and that afternoon we got her to agree to go to "memory camp." We told her it was a place that would help her with her memory, that there'd be specialists, that it would be good for her.

Yes, we tricked her. And no, we didn't think we were being clever. We were at our wits' end and she would never have stepped through the door of a "memory care" facility.

Two little letters.

A great big difference.

My sister and I drove her to "camp" together. And we could feel her suspicion growing as we guided her to the front door. This looked nothing like the camps she'd dropped us off at when we were kids. What was this place?

She hesitated.

Then held back.

My sister and I exchanged glances. *Uh-oh.*

And then the director came out, charmed Mom, eased her over the threshold and inside. We told Mom we'd see her soon, and as she was led away to a music activity that was about to begin, my sister and I escaped to Mom's room to deliver some final things and make sure everything was set.

Minutes later we were finished up and about to leave when we heard someone squalling.

"Is that Mom?" my sister asked, and sure enough, Mom had already escaped the music activity, stating loudly that she was "not interested in that noise."

Which left us stuck in her room, acting like a couple of terrified mice. How were we going to get out of there without her seeing us? Mom was suffering from memory loss, but she was no dummy. And now that she was in the common area and had seen the other residents, she was surely realizing that this "memory camp" looked suspiciously like an old folks' home!

After some clandestine maneuvering, which involved the assistant director, the back-garden pathway, and a master key, we did eventually escape the facility, but I had trouble escaping the guilt.

Memory camp.

Mom had trusted me!

Was I a terrible daughter?

My husband reminded me again and again that we really had exhausted every other option. But still, there was guilt.

After the required first week of no contact, he and I began what would become two years of visiting her almost every day.

In the beginning, visits would take hours. We would make sure she got a walk, we'd sit and eat with her and participate in activities. There was no "slipping out" until she was ready for a nap. In the moment, she knew exactly what was going on, but half an hour after we'd left, she wouldn't remember that we'd visited. But she also, thankfully, didn't know how long she'd been at camp. When she was asked, her guess was "Two weeks?" when in reality it had been months.

At some point during our visits, my husband and I would "do the rounds"—have a quick visit with other residents in the common area. As Mom's condition progressed and she spent more time sleeping, we spent more time hanging out with the other residents, and, not seeing their own families—or not having family to see—they adopted us.

There was the woman from Oklahoma who thought I was her daughter and told me the same thing every single day: "Y'all drive safe, y'hear?" There was the woman who had met Frank Sinatra and would recount the experience again and again like it had just happened. There was the woman who loved me "to pieces" and asked me every day, "Do you belong to me?"

And then there was the woman who had absolutely no interest in me but lit up when she saw my husband. "Yoo-hoo!" she'd call to him from across the room, and if he got too close, she'd give a wicked grin, grab his backside, and *squeeze*.

At ninety-two, she still had it going on.

As time went by, I witnessed so many things at this place.

I saw my mom in a walker war with another resident, both women yelling and yanking from opposite ends. I saw her flirt with a new roommate from her hospice bed, mistakenly thinking the new resident was a man. I saw accidents of all kinds, watched dentures fly, tempers flare, and residents appear from their room overjoyed by the freedom of being buck naked.

Perhaps most amazing to me was seeing that people who can no longer read or do simple arithmetic or dress themselves can somehow remember with frightening clarity who gets to sit with them at meals and activities and who doesn't. Even in a memory care facility where nobody remembers a thing, mean girls still rule.

It was also a little mind-blowing to reconcile the residents as they were now with the stories that unfolded about them. The lives they'd lived. The careers they'd had. The academic degrees they held.

During all our time there, we got to know and really appreciate the caregivers, too. What a job. Lifting residents, changing their diapers, bathing them, doing their laundry, feeding them, mopping up their messes . . . all while trying to stay upbeat and calm when food or teeth or tempers went flying. It didn't take long for us to be in awe of the way they could defuse a tense situation, redirect a resident away from tears, or wield a lipstick and cooing compliments to make a senior feel beautiful.

When my mom passed away, she seemed to be at peace with her environment, which is saying something. The staff there had a lot to do with that, and I developed an abiding gratitude for the way they helped us transition through a really emotional and difficult time. But it wasn't until the week after Mom died and I was delivering a thank-you lunch to the staff that I realized how much I had learned and felt during those two years. Perhaps it was that final goodbye and reminiscing about Mom and the things we'd seen and been through together, but I left that day thinking that maybe I could say thank you in a way that was more meaningful than a lunch.

I also started to consider that, despite this having been a mostly adult experience, despite the sadness that surrounded it, there was a broader story here. One that could, perhaps, open a window into this secluded world. One that might let some fresh air and sunlight in for people who'd been through something similar.

And, maybe more important, for those who hadn't.

# 42

## THE SECRET LIFE OF LINCOLN JONES

Humor was the life raft that kept us from drowning in the stress, helplessness, and heartache of Mom's decline. Humor also served to make things less traumatic for our kids. Old ladies fighting over a walker became dinnertime tales of "walker wars." Flying dentures and senior food fights and mean-girl antics got spun into stories with a humorous twist. The residents got nicknames; so did the caregivers. Even when they hadn't been able to visit Mom for a while, our sons knew all the players, as well as their personalities and quirks. So when they *did* visit, they were up to speed on palace intrigue and knew what to watch for.

Especially "Yoo-hoo!" from across the room.

What also helped us, I think, was the frequency of our visits. I know people who say they don't do hospitals. Or old folks' homes. Then they go on and on about the smell and the trauma of being surrounded by death.

And yeah. There is all that. And yeah. It's hard. And yeah, the first time you go, all you're thinking about is leaving. But being there is actually *not* about you. And if you "do" hospitals and you "do" old folks' homes enough, your role as someone who brings comfort overrides the discomfort of being there.

When a story suitable for young readers set in a memory care facility began forming in my mind, I replayed the evolution of my own understanding and attitude, as well as those of my kids. And what kept bubbling to the surface were two basic things:

First, finding humor in the situation was essential.

And second, conveying this one crucial concept was key: People in elder care don't want to be in their condition. People in elder care once led active, vibrant lives. People in elder care were once children, too.

When I'd summoned the courage to *not* leave the past two years behind, what poured out of me was *The Secret Life of Lincoln Jones*—the story of a sixth-grade boy who has to spend his after-school hours at a dementia care facility where his mother works as a caregiver. Lincoln is already at a disadvantage because he's the new kid at school and already harboring secrets besides that his mother has a job "changin' oldies' diapers."

As I did writing *How I Survived Being a Girl*, and as authors often do, I incorporated fictionalized versions of events and personalities into the story. But, as stories *always* do, Lincoln's story morphed into one he experienced, not me. The events and setting are seen through his eyes, which became a whole new and fascinating perspective to consider. What would daily visits to a dementia care facility be like for a sixth grader? What would his presence be like for the residents? What would it take for Lincoln to truly get that these "oldies" were once sixth graders too?

People have asked which character in *Lincoln Jones* is my mother, but it didn't work that way. My mom's personality, feistiness, stubbornness, *quirkiness* couldn't be contained by one character. There's a little of her in several of the characters, including (forgive me, Mom) the Psychic Vampire in Room 102.

And that's all I'm gonna say about *that*.

Now, while I divvied my mom's traits into several characters, Lincoln's mother is a composite of the people—the angels, really—who cared for my mom during the last two years of her life. There are many facets to *The Secret Life of Lincoln Jones*, but one I really hope shines through is the tribute to caregivers for the hard job they do.

So sometimes a story can build inside you without your even being aware that it's there. Sometimes you collect pieces and subconsciously store them away, totally unaware of how or why they belong together. Sometimes you can't see the story because you're too busy trying to hold the real world together. And sometimes you don't notice it under all your baggage.

But always when you find it, it will teach you to look at the world with new eyes, and in the process, it will show you ways to let that baggage go.

# 43

# BRIDGE OUT

Family vacations when I was a kid consisted of camping. I'm sure economics had a lot to do with that. And since gas was cheap back then, camping was the end part of long days on the road in our parents' International Harvester—a large, chrome-bumpered precursor to today's SUV. With its V-8 engine and heavy steel construction, it probably got a whopping twelve miles to the gallon on the highway. Add six people, a good-sized dog, a top carrier stuffed with supplies, and more necessities wedged into traditional and created spaces inside (like under Dad-built backseat benches placed where legs were designed to dangle), and that mileage had to be somewhere in the single digits.

On road trips we often headed east from our home in the Los Angeles area. Later, we also spent time backpacking through the picturesque Sierra Nevada mountains, but what I remember most from my ten-and-under years are long, hot stretches of desert as we drove around Southern California, Arizona, Utah, and Nevada without air-conditioning.

This was pre-internet, and pre-GPS, and pre-men-not-being-opposed-to-asking-for-directions.

This was also pre-screen-entertainment, so we kids did a lot of spotting out-of-state license plates, shared a rotation of already-read comic books, and ignored instructions to "look at the beautiful scenery."

We also did a lot of jockeying for space, which often escalated from jabbing elbows to throwing fists, and somewhere on every trip Dad resorted to the pull-over-and-spank routine.

Burning buns and tears in an overheating vehicle in the desert.

Ah, summer vacation.

What we *did* have were maps and guidebooks and a quirky mother who liked to get off the beaten path. We also had a dad who didn't believe signs that said things like BRIDGE OUT or ROAD CLOSED or DANGER. Weatherworn or barely legible, these were obviously old advisories. And even when the paint was fresh and said in no uncertain terms TURN BACK (YES, THIS MEANS YOU, MISTER WITH THE WIFE AND FOUR KIDS AND FURRY DOG), Dad had the, uh, *gumption* to press ahead, just in case. After all, the crisp new map he'd purchased at the gas station clearly showed this road was fine.

Dirt, maybe, but fine.

Besides, the return route was long and wouldn't get us to our campsite before dark.

So off we'd go. And when the bridge was indeed out, Dad

would still not be ready to throw in the towel. Perhaps we could ford the river. When closer inspection revealed a manageable water depth, boulders that weren't too big, and—wait, wait, look at that! tire tracks on both sides!—well, why not give it a whirl?

The International Harvester was not a four-wheel-drive. It was a poor, overloaded utilitarian station wagon.

So, yes, we got stuck.

Again.

That time, fortunately, a jeep happened by. It *was* a four-wheel-drive. And since our vehicle was deeply planted mid-stream and obstructing *their* ability to cross the river—or maybe just out of the kindness of their clearly inebriated hearts—they hitched a chain to our bumper and, after much grinding of gears and flinging of mud, managed to pull us back onto the dirt road.

I never needed an official lesson in how to change a tire or use a board or branches to give a wheel traction when it was digging a portal into Stucksville, or how to get down and really *push*. These were all included free in the vacation package. As were fire-building and latrine-digging and tent-pitching and water-hauling.

I look back in true amazement that we all survived. After all, it's hard to keep an eye on four kids when you're trying to rev your way out of a steep ravine, and maybe it's easy to lose track of the one behind a back wheel who's still putting her heart and soul into the heave-ho as the car slides back in.

But once we got to camp, all the getting-there was forgotten.

We were free-range kids, scampering off in some middle-of-nowhere place to find firewood or just explore.

Or get lost.

But there's always echolocation to find your way back, right? You holler something. Preferably not "Help," as your dad has sternly instructed you that "Help" conveys the wrong message when you're simply lost. So even though "Help!" is really what you want to shout, you call out something like "Where are you?" And when someone finally hears you and hollers back "Here!" you holler "*Where?*" Then they holler "Here!" but you still can't find them, so you holler "WHERE?" and they holler "HERE!" and so it goes until you finally find your way back to camp, only to get scolded for not sticking together with your brothers, who may or may not have ditched you, depending on who you ask.

Still. The being-in-a-campground stuff was mostly great. Well, except that time we set up camp at the aptly named Valley of Fire, Nevada, in the middle of July, where the average temperature for that time of year is 106 degrees Fahrenheit. I don't know if what led us there was an aversion to nearby Las Vegas or that the guidebook boasted of stunning geology and un-rivaled views, but please take my word for it: You do not want to camp at the Valley of Fire in the summertime.

Anyway, aside from being ditched or sun-baked, the camping part of our vacation *was* usually great. And, ironically, the places we wound up because we got stuck or lost were actually the best. There wasn't an assigned campsite where you had to park and pitch your tent, there were no neighbor campers squirting lighter fluid directly into a burning fire (Mom's pet peeve), nobody played a radio too loud (Dad's) or got in embarrassing fights or stayed up 'til "all hours" partying (oh, the things we learned!). After dinner and KP, it was just us in our big canvas tent, tucked in and tired, playing Animal, Vegetable, Mineral in the dark until one by one we fell asleep.

As we got older, our family switched to backpacking. Likely to get away from the campground crowds. We had some gorgeous packing adventures through the Sierra Nevada mountains, where just the sweet smell of ponderosa pines is enough to keep you going. Tired of hiking? Stop and smell the sappy trunk of a ponderosa. It's a little whiff of heaven.

When we moved away from Los Angeles, backpacking adventures shifted to treks through the Los Padres National Forest. Don't let the word *forest* fool you. The Los Padres wilderness is covered in scratchy chaparral, where ticks and maddening little flies are plentiful and water sources are not. And yet, we hiked it. Year after year. And as we kids moved into adulthood, we continued to backpack on our own—with each other, with Scouts, or with friends. I look back at all the endless miles I've hiked with a pack on my back—all the blisters and bugs and discomfort . . . and I ask myself, Why?

I don't know if it was a yearning for something, or just habit, but I can honestly say that the years of camping and backpacking did equip me in ways I continue to recognize. And despite the discomfort and the fights and the follies of Bridge-Out situations, there will always be magic in the memory of falling asleep in a big canvas tent surrounded by family, a cool breeze on my face as I looked up at the stars in a middle-of-nowhere sky.

## 44

WILD BIRD

Camping and nature first found their way into my writing in *Sammy Keyes and the Wild Things,* where our reluctant heroine goes on her first backpacking trip with some overzealous Girl Scouts. Sammy gets exposed to all manner of nasty beasties—gnatty flies, scorpions, ticks, rattlesnakes, and wild boars (welcome to the Los Padres National Forest)—as well as the joys of summer camping in harsh environs, all for the chance to spot an endangered condor. The story is a backdoor approach to environmentalism, with Sammy at first wondering why in the world anyone would want to save an enormous ugly bird that poops itself to cool down and feasts on dead stuff.

Boy, did I have a lot of fun writing that one. (Including getting to see—up close and within smelling distance—the release of a rehabilitated condor into the wild.)

But camping was just the setting there. The chance to put Sammy "up a tree" (in this case one with "sudden oak death," which, cross my heart, is a real and dangerous thing) and throw rocks (and ticks and gnatty flies and scorpions and wild boars and condor poachers) at her.

The role of camping in the story didn't go any deeper than that.

And then one night . . .

I was catching up with a friend I'd been out of touch with for a few years and she told me she'd made the excruciating decision to send her child to a wilderness therapy camp.

The wilderness as therapy?

Was that like going for walks in the woods? Maybe with a yoga mat?

Not even close. This wilderness therapy camp turned out to be a minimalist camp in the Utah desert, an immersive program where troubled youths between thirteen and eighteen were isolated and stripped of outside influences in an effort to bring them back from self-destructive behaviors and onto a better path.

I started asking other people if they'd heard of wilderness therapy camps, and to my surprise the answer was often yes. What's more, several volunteered that they personally knew someone who had sent their out-of-control teen to one.

This was mind-blowing to me. Parents had their kids "kidnapped" in the middle of the night for this? Really? And paid a ton of money for it?

So I started digging, and a picture began to emerge of what teens sent to Utah wilderness therapy camps were in for: six to eight weeks in the desert, forced to cope with Mother Nature's unbending will, forced to start a fire with friction, construct their own shelter, cook meals over an open flame, purify water from natural sources, dig latrines, and honor the earth.

Wow.

Sounded a lot like growing up Van Draanen to me.

It was then that my often-disgruntled view of time spent camping in the desert shifted. The value of becoming competent in wilderness survival as a way to help you navigate through life and your own internal storms came into focus. If it's on you to start your own fire, find your own water, build your own shelter . . . if you have to suffer the consequences of not doing these things, eventually you'll get hungry enough, or thirsty enough, or weatherworn enough to look for solutions. And once the blame game has gotten you nowhere and you recognize that Mother Nature is unmoved by your tantrums or misery and that your success or failure is the direct result of the effort you apply, you will begin to try.

You may be totally ticked off while you're trying, but that doesn't matter—whatever it takes. Because effort is the first step in making a change.

And with that change will eventually come success.

And with success will come the feeling of accomplishment.

And with accomplishment will come empowerment.

Pretty soon your thoughts will move from *I can't* (or *I don't want to*) to *I can (so get out of my way)*.

The more competent, the more empowered. The more empowered, the more fearless.

Like a bolt of lightning through a desert sky, desert

camping—desert survival—was suddenly something worth exploring, not as a setting, but as an agent of change.

And quickly following that bolt of lightning was a rumble of thunder:

During my first six years of full-time teaching, I worked two nights a week at a continuation high school trying to help at-risk teens get their GED. The reasons these teens had landed at the continuation school varied widely from apathy to drug use to pregnancy, but the goal of each student was the same: finish high school because . . . because they needed to because . . . because everyone said they needed a diploma to get anywhere in life.

Which is, by and large, true in our society. But for most of these students, much bigger issues were at play in their lives. Almost all of them needed repeated pep talks, because they could see no relevance to many of the courses required for graduating. Were they ever going to use the quadratic formula? Almost certainly not. But even more crucial than curriculum concerns, these were teens adrift. They were already way off course, but worse, they hadn't found a passion that could pull them back. Without an internal fire to keep them motivated, what chance did they have?

Suddenly these two threads that had woven through my life—camping and working with at-risk kids—tied unexpectedly together in the square knot of *Wild Bird,* the story of Wren Clemmens, a girl who's gone so far off the rails that, in a move of desperation, her parents have her taken against her will to wilderness therapy camp in the Utah desert. It's the story of learning to build a fire to survive in the wild, and also of learning to build a fire inside your heart, to find a passion that will give you a reason to move forward through life in a positive way.

*Wild Bird* was a story I'd been preparing for my entire life without knowing it. It just took one strand of a friend's experience to open up the possibility for seemingly unrelated threads to be woven together in a meaningful way.

What this underscores is that when you grow up with something or are surrounded by it, you often don't recognize the value in it. I certainly didn't appreciate the "beautiful scenery" at the time. But maybe it was all the crazy camping and Bridge Out experiences that gave me the, uh, *gumption* to think I could change a clutch, which made me think I could help rebuild a factory, which made me think that, by comparison, how hard could getting published be?

You just can't know how what you've been through (or what you're going through) will prepare you or equip you with something you'll need in the future. The relevance may unfold in short order, or it may take years, but your experiences are all seeds. So collect them. Store them for when the time is right. They will let you know when it's their time to sprout.

# A PEEK BEHIND
# THE CURTAIN

---

# 45

# BECAUSE YOU ASKED

When I became a published author, I knew very little about how the business end of publishing worked, or even what the process of bookmaking was beyond the point at which a manuscript was accepted. And the questions I get asked most by aspiring writers indicate that they're floating around in that same boat.

Clearly this book is not a how-to manual for getting published. My hope is that it's helpful to you as a writer and as a *person*. But I've spent many years of interacting with writers—and those just beginning to think about becoming one—and there is no ignoring their desire to know more about publishing.

There are also, I've found, a lot of misconceptions about the process and the roles of the people who are involved in turning writers' words into books. So in this section I'll touch on the basics and answer the questions I get asked again and again, as well as relate a few stories that may shed a little light on the process as a whole.

Remember, this is not a how-to, just a peek behind the curtain. But I do hope you find it useful!

## 46

## PUBLISHING LIMBO

In publishing, there can be long stretches of slipping gears, interrupted by the rev of something happening, followed by the quick drop into neutral. (I'm pressing the gas, why am I not going anywhere? No! Please don't make me change the clutch!)

Back in the Box House, while my potential editor was "waiting for the time to be right" to present *Girl* to her new editor in chief before she could offer me a contract, I continued working on *Sammy Keyes and the Skeleton Man*.

An element of naïveté might be necessary when pursuing big dreams. Like thinking it's a good idea to write a second title without a contract for the first. But working on Sammy's story made sense to me. And it felt good to continue to put hope in the mail.

But when I started forming ideas for a *third* Sammy Keyes book and I still didn't have a contract for *anything*, I finally mustered the nerve to call the editor who had *Girl*. Was it ever going to be "the right time"?

I had not spoken in person to any editor or agent before and didn't know what to expect. Was calling a faux pas? Was she going to be brusque and annoyed? Or, worse, would it roll over to voice mail, where I would undoubtedly make a babbling fool of myself?

But I'd just had a birthday and was sure not getting any younger. So I steeled my nerves and dialed.

My heart went into overdrive when she answered the phone. I told her who I was, and to my utter amazement she said, "Oh, Wendelin! I'm glad you called. I just got out of a meeting and I have great news!"

She then made an offer on *How I Survived Being a Girl*, and just like that, after ten years of trying, the waiting was over.

After we hung up, I floated around, living on cloud nine.

Finally!

But what followed the joyful acceptance phone call was the anxious waiting for a contract. When, after six weeks, it finally arrived, I read it and realized that, having no agent to guide me, I was way out of my league. I didn't know what was standard or what might constitute foolish giveaways on my part.

The advance I'd been offered was quite modest, but I was well beyond caring about big money. I just wanted a real book. One I could hold in my hands. One I could go to the library and check out.

But I didn't want to be a chump, either. So I did a little research, then drove an hour to meet with an entertainment lawyer. He was the closest thing I could find to a book-publishing attorney in my area, and his secretary had assured me he was familiar with publishing contracts.

Ironically, going to see him was what made me a chump. He clearly knew less about it than I did, and I got billed two hours for what boiled down to "Looks good."

So I compiled a list of my own questions, called the editor, and tried to not let on how nervous I was in questioning some points of the contract.

She was pleasant and receptive, explaining why she couldn't change some things and agreeing to compromise on others. I signed the amended contract and returned it, and then began the anxious wait for the countersigned contract and manuscript revision notes to arrive.

Meanwhile, once again, I got back to work.

I finished Sammy #3.

There was no word from New York.

I couldn't stop the creeping doubts. Had something gone wrong?

Determined to stay productive, I began Sammy #4.

Finally, the revision process for *Girl* began, which, as you know, I found to be torturous. There was some contact with my editor during that time, but when the revision was complete, once again, things went quiet.

Again, I tried to stay productive and returned to writing. But when the silence was finally broken, I wished it hadn't been. I learned that the publication for *Girl* had been delayed for a season and that the book was now "orphaned" because my editor was leaving her job at the *Girl* publishing house for an editorial position at Knopf.

It was no longer my imagination. I *was* on very shaky ground.

So, okay. You already know that *Girl* was eventually published, and that my editor and I have worked happily ever after. The point of this story is that the road to publication can be bumpy and full of potholes, but no matter how rough the process becomes, make yourself move ahead with your writing.

Create possibility.

Keep putting hope in the mail.

Because even if that deal you've waited a decade for falls through, you'll have a body of work waiting to catch you.

## 47

---

# THE DAY I MET MY EDITOR

Over six years after she'd asked me to cut *How I Survived Being a Girl* in half, my editor and I finally had the chance to meet in person at a writers' conference in Southern California. We'd been invited to be on a panel to discuss the editor-author relationship and she was flying in from New York for it. I was really excited to meet her, and also more than a little nervous.

The second Sammy Keyes was soon to be released, so we'd worked our way through three books at this point and I felt like I knew her. But people can be quite different in person than they are through written correspondence, or even over the phone. Would it be weird? Awkward? Would she hate me?

Also, she'd gathered information about me for promotional purposes, along with a head shot. But since this was pre-social-media-explosion, I didn't even know what she looked like!

This was my first writers' conference and I didn't have high expectations for accommodations, but I was still a little disappointed to find that I'd be sharing a small room with two other authors, and that, being the newbie and the last to arrive, I got the rollaway cot.

The other two authors were new friends to me and were great. Encouraging and supportive and fun to be around, they'd known each other a long time and had both been successfully published for many years. They seemed to enjoy showing me the ropes, and it was in this little motel room that they seeded the idea of my doing school visits, assuring me that I could make a living that way.

I was skeptical. None of the schools I'd attended as a kid had ever hosted an author. The first time I met a real live author was after I'd been published. Schools would pay you to visit?

They were elaborating when the motel phone rang. It was my editor.

"I'm going over to her room," I said after I hung up.

They knew I was nervous. "She will love you!" they called as I scurried out the door.

I remember my first impression of my best friend from grad school. I thought she was a snob. Her first impression of me? She thought I was a ditz. (So I'm blond and have retained my inner child. Judge some?) The point being, first impressions can be damning, and I'm glad my friend and I got to a point where we could share our first thoughts about each other and laugh over how wrong we were.

The same would be true of meeting my editor.

She opened the door to her room and (she later told me)

thought, *Eating disorder?* I took one look at her and thought, *Whoa! My editor is Snow White.*

And I suddenly felt like a giant.

I'm a little shy of six feet tall.

My editor is barely five.

What my friend and editor share (aside from wrong first impressions of me) is a way of making me feel like we've been friends since childhood. They both give me an easy sense of connection, of being understood, and beyond that—and just as important—they both make me laugh. I mean, really, really laugh.

Before long, my editor and I had moved past first-meeting formalities and were facing each other crisscross-applesauce across the gap between her room's two queen beds. I couldn't help bouncing on the mattress a little. (You try not bouncing if you're ever crisscross-applesaucing with Snow White.)

The conversation wound around all over the place, from personal stuff, to the great reception we'd been getting for the first two Sammys, to the upcoming Sammys that were slated for publication, to the next Sammy under revision. Sammy, Sammy, Sammy. It was so much fun to talk to someone (aside from my husband) who also spoke about Sammy Keyes like she was real. Actually, it was . . . awesome.

Finally we began discussing strategies for the next day's conference panel. The topic was the editor-author relationship—how I'd found her, what it was about my writing that had caught her attention, how the revision process worked for us . . . that sort of thing.

And this is when she broke it to me.

The reason everything had taken so long.

The truth about *Girl* almost not being published.

"She hated it," my editor said about a newly hired boss's reaction to *Girl*. "She wanted to cancel the contract."

My editor had fought for the book and had won, but a bunch of other stuff came out then too. And I suddenly understood that her path hadn't been an easy one either. While I'd been feeling ignored or neglected, she'd been trying to shield me from in-house turmoil. "I didn't want you to worry," she explained.

In return I explained that I'd rather know what was going on than wonder. Because when you wonder, you start imagining all sorts of bad outcomes, which can wind up being worse than any actual bad outcome.

Although I couldn't really think of an outcome that would have been worse than having *Girl* dropped from the list.

After everything I'd been through?

Yeah, that would have been devastating.

This was a conference of aspiring kid-lit authors and illustrators. And it was clear from the accommodations (her two queens to our crammed two-twins-plus-a-cot) that guest editors were more highly valued participants than authors. (Which made sense, I guess. The authors had what the conference attendees wanted—we could even be viewed as competition—whereas the editors were the ones who could make their publishing dreams come true.)

So when my editor asked who I was staying with and I let

on that there were three of us in a room half the size of hers, she invited me to share her room. And normally I would never have taken her up on it, but what came out of my mouth was "Really?"

"Of course," she said, reading my thoughts. "Don't be silly. Go get your stuff."

So I did.

Now, the reason I've told you this story is to illustrate the importance of finding an editor who is right for *you*. There are a lot of editors in publishing, and some of them will hate your work or want to cut you off at the knees when you've barely learned to stand.

Others will understand you.

They may even like you.

The former is more important than the latter, but the combination—if you're lucky enough to find it—is something to treasure.

Which brings us to this story's sequel.

A sequel that's all about . . . a sequel.

## 48

THE SEQUEL ABOUT A SEQUEL

One of the things my editor told me during our sleepover heart-to-heart was that her accepting a job at Knopf was partly driven by her wanting to buy Sammy Keyes. She hadn't been able to offer a contract while at the other house because the thinking there was "Let's see how *Girl* does first," bridging toward a tepid "Maybe try just one" approach to Sammy. Which is why that whole "Start with *Skeleton Man*" idea was suggested.

While my editor was, unbeknownst to me, planning to switch houses, I had retained an agent. A single-book contract mistake is one thing; making avoidable errors on a series deal is another. And since, in my mind, Sammy Keyes was a series, I wanted an agent to do the contracts for Sammy.

But those contracts weren't offered. And since there was no indication as to why, my agent started shopping Sammy around.

I was forthright with my editor about it, and although it didn't make her happy, she didn't try to stop me. If I had known what she was going through, I would have thought better of it, but all I knew was that I'd completed four books in a series that seemed stuck in limbo. (If I could encourage one thing, it would be for people to *talk to each other*.)

Then my editor switched houses, and since her new position gave her more authority and freedom, one of her first calls was to see if Sammy was still available. My agent immediately put the brakes on shopping the books elsewhere, and things fell together pretty quickly after that.

Then Sammy Keyes shot out of the gate by winning an Edgar for *Hotel Thief*, and weird stuff started happening. People in publishing who had turned me down for years were now knocking. Would I be interested in writing a mystery for *them*? Would I consider contributing to their mystery anthology? One even asked me if I'd write a foreword to a Sherlock Holmes collection for kids.

Sherlock Holmes?

Really?

I was like, *I am so not qualified to do that!* But I didn't tell *them* that. I simply replied with what they'd been telling *me* for years: *I'm sorry. This is not right for me at this time. But please. Think of me again with your next project.*

But the biggest jaw-drop happened at another conference that I was attending courtesy of Knopf. My editor was there too, in charge of making sure her authors got to the publisher's floor booth and sessions and other functions on time. The one thing she didn't shepherd me to was a dinner I'd been invited to by the *Girl* house.

"Really?" she asked when I told her about the invitation, and she seemed a little backcombed about it, although she did her best to hide it. After all, she was attending a dinner with one of her other authors . . . something I'd realized I needed to adapt to with grace. (Authors may have only one editor, but editors must, by the nature of their job, juggle several authors' books at once.)

"I have no idea why," I told her, and in my mind it was a simple matter of *Girl* being on their list and them knowing I'd be at the conference.

Which was all it seemed to be until midway through the meal, when the editor who'd been assigned to take over *Girl* duties told me that they were interested in . . .

A sequel to *Girl*.

It's a good thing I hadn't just taken a bite because I would have sprayed it. How could they want a sequel when they almost hadn't published the original?

The boss there hated it!

Plus, I didn't see a sequel. I liked the way *Girl* ended. Maybe I was too close to it. Maybe the story line was too much like my childhood's. Maybe I was in my own way. But in that moment, I couldn't see where a sequel might take the story.

But what flashed through my mind was that it would be interesting—cool, and really funny, actually—to have a story from the neighbor *boy's* point of view. It could be *How I Survived Being a Boy . . . (In a Neighborhood with That Girl)* and chronicle the same time frame as *Girl*, only from the neighbor boy's perspective.

The idea tickled my brain, so I shared it with the editor as an alternate idea, but she politely dismissed it and said they were interested in a traditional sequel.

I told her I'd give it some thought, but the more I thought about it, the more closed to the idea I became. So much about it felt wrong, and my mind was still reeling.

A sequel?

To a book they'd hated?

After dinner, I admit it: I phoned my editor, then zipped up to her room. Once again, we were crisscross-applesauce and I was spilling what had happened.

She was calm. Kind. Gracious. "You can do it, Wendelin. If you want to, go ahead."

"But why do they want a sequel? It doesn't make sense. They didn't even like *Girl*."

So she explained to me that *Girl* had already "earned out" (more on this later), and with an Edgar on my mantel, I was now an award winner with a series they'd missed out on. Clearly, she said, I had a really bright future.

Sitting there hearing this, I remember feeling the blinders come off.

Oh. It was business.

It wasn't the story, it was the success.

Something about hearing this was kind of crushing. What about craft? What about story? My mind snapped back to the years of rejection, to trying to break in, to moving past financial considerations and just wanting someone, somewhere, to love my writing enough to give it a chance.

And then, the revelation.

Crisscross-applesauce across from me was the one person who had given me that chance. And in that moment I knew that this was more than business to me. She was the one who'd brought me to this dance; it'd be wrong to cut out or flit around.

So even though she'd said it was okay to write a sequel to *Girl*, I was done with the idea. "I'm not going to do it," I told her. But since it was still tickling my brain, I told her my idea for *Boy*.

She thought it was charming, with lots of potential. "Maybe *we* could publish it?"

We both pondered that for a moment, but it was clearly an idea rife with potential problems.

"I could start all over?" I suggested. "Tell a story from both a girl's side and a boy's side?"

"You could," she agreed.

And a few years later, I did just that, writing the book that became *Flipped*.

# 49

## FIRST ARRIVAL

So what's it like, holding your first book for the very first time?

For many it's magical.

For me?

After ten years of waiting, I think mine's one for the books, but not in the way you might imagine.

I was on my way out the Box House door, late (as usual) getting my young children to their swimming lessons, when I noticed a FedEx mailer on my porch.

FedEx?

To someone who carefully weighed her mailings and precisely calculated postage, this seemed extravagant. Who was FedExing me?

I dead-bolted the front door and the security screen and scooped up the mailer.

Return address: my publisher!

Mailer weight and size: a book!

My heart went into overdrive. "Wait up!" I called to my kids, who were already racing toward our car at the curb. "I think this is my book!"

It was.

Only . . . it wasn't.

It had my name on the cover, but . . . but they'd changed the title!

My knees buckled. I crumpled to the porch step as I absorbed the cover.

How could they have changed the title?

I opened the book and . . . and . . . they'd also changed the words! The character names were . . . different and . . . and . . . I fanned through the pages . . . it was *so* different. How could they *do* this?

"What's wrong, Mom?" my son asked because, yes, there were tears. And because I had no words, I simply showed him the cover. And he said, "Looks like Quasimodo!"

We'd recently watched Disney's *The Hunchback of Notre Dame,* and he was right: The cartoony character on the cover of my book—the girl with the wild short hair, cockeyed face, and hugely hunched shoulder—did, indeed, look like a young, female hunchback.

I wailed, "She does!"

And he said, "Who's it supposed to be?"

And I wailed, "Me!" Because as much as I plead the Fifth, the story I'd written was a fictionalized version of my childhood, which made the main character a fictionalized version of *me*. And no, the character didn't have to look like Esmeralda—

the beautiful woman in *Hunchback*—but did they have to make
her look so much like Quasimodo?

I couldn't see anything anymore. There were tears everywhere. And somewhere in the wailing and gasping and trying
to explain, the cover came off the book and it slowly dawned on
me that I was holding . . . somebody else's book?

Yes. Somebody else's book. This *wasn't* a first copy of my
book after all. It was a different book with a mock-up of my
book's cover wrapped around it.

My editor later told me that she had sent the newly minted
jacket around another book to try to show how terrific the cover
would look. And oh—oops about the title. Hadn't she discussed
that with me?

Uh . . . *nooooooo*.

What I then learned was that people in-house thought my
title (*Walking on Sensitive Grass*) was too literary—that the book
needed a title with a lighter, more humorous feel. Apparently
my editor agreed. They made a long list of alternate titles. *How
I Survived Being a Girl* won.

It took time to embrace the look and the humor of the situation, but eventually, I did. And after innumerable compliments
on the jacket from booksellers, I stopped seeing the hunchback
and started seeing an effective cover—one that stood out and
made you want to pick up the book.

And although I still like *Walking on Sensitive Grass* better as
a title, I don't know that it would have been a more *effective* title.
Maybe the book would have bombed with that title. Or maybe
not. At the point when I learned about the change, it seemed to

be beyond discussion, so really, the only choice I had was in my reaction to it, and I chose to be gracious about it. The bottom line is, you *work* with people at your publishing house, and if you have a conniption or act like a diva, you're not going to be someone they'll want to continue to work with.

My editor was apologetic, and as I later learned, *Girl* was her first solo acquisition, so I wasn't the only one climbing the learning curve. To this day, she cringes at the memory of that oversight.

So changing the title of your book without your consent is *not* standard or something you should be worried about happening, but if something similar happens to you, step back, cool off, address the problem but keep things in perspective. Someday you'll be able to look back on the incident and laugh.

## 50

---

# EDITORS

Eons ago, I thought editors edited. You know—nipped and tucked your story and gave guidance for making it better.

And they do.

What I did not know was that editing is only a small fraction of what they do. The actual job is so broad and complex that it still leaves me scratching my head. From negotiating the terms of book contracts, to presenting books at conferences, to working with sales and marketing and publicity departments, how is one person supposed to juggle so much? As time went by, the tasks I learned were part of my editor's job kept mounting. It wasn't until I had known her for twenty years that I finally asked her to tell me everything.

You ready?

Here's what she does at her desk/in the office:

- Email. It's a biggie for all working adults, but she has to field email from all over the place. She gets questions from authors and agents; updates from marketing, publicity, and sales; book reviews; industry newsletters; notices of reprints, first prints, out-of-prints; requests for meetings; and submissions. Then, of course, there's the responding to emails: *answering* those questions from authors and agents; passing on the good and bad news; requesting information from others and then disseminating the answers.

- She prepares a case for new books that she'd like to acquire. This is a written appraisal of why the book is great, who will love it, who will buy it, how they'll pitch it in-house and out-of-house. It also includes a long-term plan for the author, an estimate of how much revision the book requires, and a profit-and-loss statement with some supportable guess of how many copies will be printed, how many will sell, what the costs to the company will be, and what the potential profit might be.
- She writes long, thoughtful letters to authors. These are always "compliment sandwiches," where she begins and ends with what's so great about your work and in between gently explains what she feels could use work while also giving constructive suggestions for how to make the book even stronger.
- She writes the copy for book jackets, sales reps' tip sheets, and online book descriptions. (After we'd

worked together for a while, she started asking me for input on some of these. They are much harder than they seem.)

- She preps manuscripts so they are in the proper format for copy editors and designers to deal with.
- She reviews books that are in progress as they're copyedited, set in type, proofread, corrected, and proofread again. And she does this as many times as it takes to get it right.
- She meets with designers to talk about the illustrations for picture books and the possibilities for jacket art for novels.
- She prepares presentations of her acquired books for meetings with sales and marketing and publicity, and different presentations for meetings with librarians and teachers, all in an effort to get them familiar with and excited about each new book.
- She attends meetings, meetings, and more meetings. First she prepares; afterward she follows up.
- She talks on the phone with agents and authors and colleagues.
- After acquisitions are approved, she negotiates the terms for new contracts with agents.
- She also meets with authors, agents, and foreign publishers who have made appointments. (In my experience, this takes *time*, including a tour through the office where you get introduced to the team

of people in-house. And despite all of the many facets of her workday, she has a way of making you feel like you're the most important thing she's got going on.)

What she "rarely, if ever" does in the office is read (submissions or revisions) or edit. That's right. With all the other aspects of her job taking up so much of the day, she winds up doing the manuscript reading and editing during off hours and weekends.

What I have come to see is that editors—not just mine—are all in. They love what they do and devote themselves to making a difference with the books they put out. From picture books to young adult novels, mine acquires about twelve manuscripts a year, and each one is special and important to her.

And now, knowing what all is involved in the job an editor does, I have a little more understanding of why things seem to take so long, why some things slip through the cracks, and why one of the best traits you can cultivate as a writer is patience.

# 51

## AGENTS

One of the most common questions I get asked by writers interested in getting a book traditionally published is *Do I need an agent?*

The realistic answer to that question is yes.

It's not the definitive answer, but your chances of placing a work of fiction with a traditional publisher are much better with an agent than without one. Editors rely on agents to find the best—most gripping, publishable, or marketable— manuscripts being sent around by authors. Reputable agents have connections to people inside publishing and know which editors may be interested in the type of thing you've written.

So an agent can greatly increase the odds of at least getting your manuscript read by editors, and they can negotiate to improve the numbers of an offer and the language in your contract. However, there is no guarantee that agent representation will actually result in an offer from an editor. There are thousands of manuscripts looking for homes. Your role in all of this is to write something that will stand out in that flood of pages. Do not underestimate the value of the *work*. Having contacts is helpful, but it's the *work* that will end up doing the talking. Make sure it's your best effort and has something compelling to say.

The catch-22 of the agent representation thing is that it can be almost as difficult to land an agent as it is to find an editor, but it has become more and more difficult to find an editor without an agent connecting you, and many publishers won't look at unagented manuscripts anymore.

Again, your best chance of getting an offer for representation is if your work really stands out. The bottom line is, if an agent reads it and loves it, she or he will be excited by the possibility of placing it.

So, okay. Let's say you believe you've written a great story. You're ready to try to place it. How do you find an agent who's right for you?

This is not a how-to guide for that, but I can say one thing for certain: A good author-agent relationship is a partnership. Beyond my agent looking out for my interests, I've relied on her many times for advice, insight, and just moral support. Go in with the optimistic view that you'll be working together for a long time, with your agent being your home base when working with what might become multiple editors at various publishing houses (since most authors don't necessarily have a single editor or a relationship with only one publishing house). Ideally, you want an agent whom you like personally as well as professionally. The publishing industry can be a roller-coaster ride, and it's nice to have someone to scream with you through unexpected drops and help keep your career on track.

So don't just send your query to Friendly-Sounding Agent or blanket Manhattan with emails. Do your homework and scout out agents who seem like they'd be right for you. It's not hard to find out who represented or edited a book you think compares to yours. (For starters, online searches and digging into the book's acknowledgments can prove to be very fruitful.) And most agents have a social media presence you can use to glean lots of information about them.

When you feel you've found someone suitable, send them a personalized query (there are a slew of resources out there to guide you in writing a query letter—study them!) and the odds of them requesting a sample of your story will go up.

Social media can also be a good way to get a heads-up on what an agent (or editor) is looking for. Especially someone who has recently joined an agency or been promoted. In their new position, they're excited to make their own mark in the industry, and sometimes they'll put a call out on social for something specific. So follow and listen.

Even though I was concerned about making a contractual mistake with the Sammy Keyes series, I was still a little on the fence about retaining an agent. Wasn't the hard part finding an editor? And since I was pretty sure I'd already done that, why would I give a percentage of everything to an agent? So before I retained my agent, I found a polite way of asking her exactly that.

After making a case for herself, she arranged for me to speak to a couple of her clients. Of course these were authors who were happy with her representation, but still, not knowing much of anything about the business of publishing, I was surprised to learn of the number of ways agency representation can benefit an author.

So, although agencies vary, here's what I hope is a helpful list of the main things a full-service firm is likely to provide for their authors:

- Some literary agents will make editorial suggestions to help get your manuscript into submission-worthy shape, while others may offer less specific or broader market advice.
- Once your agent thinks your manuscript is one they can place, they will shop it to editors they believe may be a good fit for your work. (A successful agent will have many contacts and personal relationships within the publishing industry.)
- They will regularly follow up with those editors, doing their best to keep things on a timely track.
- When an editor makes an offer, the agent will negotiate the terms of the contract. (This includes the advance payment, the payment schedule, royalty rates, and exactly which rights will go to the publisher and which will be retained by the author.)
- The agency may have a film subagent or a film rights department that will work to place your

book as a screen property (basically doing all of the above regarding rights and payments, only as a film property instead of a book).

- They may have a foreign rights department and/or subagents throughout the world who will pitch your book to foreign markets (and negotiate and collect, etc.).
- They will handle other unsold ancillary rights.
- The agency tracks and collects all moneys owed to you, and disburses them to you (minus their commission), while providing a full accounting of all payments. With the financial details centered in one place, an agency is a great resource when accounting questions arise.
- An experienced agent can also provide overall career guidance (which is increasingly important, considering the complexity and ongoing evolution of today's publishing landscape). They are the author's advocate and ally, especially when there are issues within the publishing house that need to be addressed.

Bottom line: If you decide to seek representation, make sure what you're looking for in an agent is included in the services they and their agency provide. Use the list here to craft some questions for them, and be sure to also ask detailed questions about the agent's methods (like their response time to emails and calls, their transparency, preferred practices, etc.).

Last suggestion, and something I wish I'd done: Get educated about the industry. Read, investigate, absorb. And attend writers' conferences where editors and agents are faculty members. Listen to what they have to say. Find ones who are looking for the sort of thing you write. It's always a plus if a query you send later mentions that you met them at a conference. And once you have an agent, it can be helpful to pass along to them information you've gathered about editors you've met or heard speak who are looking for the sort of thing you've written.

And please. If you get turned down, don't be discouraged. Understand that it's just part of the process, and that the way forward is to try, try again. Keep at it consistently, persistently, and for exactly as long as it takes. Being armed with this fundamental knowledge should definitely help speed things up.

# 52

## COPY EDITORS

What's a copy editor, and how does a copy editor differ from an editor?

The copy editor's job begins after the author and editor have gone back and forth on a manuscript and have revised it to a point where they both feel it's in great shape and is ready for a different kind of scrutiny.

My (usually) affectionate name for the copy editor who weighs in on one of my manuscripts is the Comma Queen. They are not all women, but I don't usually know who the copy editor is on any given project, so whenever I'm in the throes of their notes, I call them the Comma Queen.

They. Are. Precise.

And it can be so maddening!

Although their titles seem similar, the copy editor's job is quite different from the editor's job. It doesn't matter if the copy editor likes your book (although when they say they do, it's always nice). It doesn't matter if they think it makes a worthwhile contribution to literature. Their focus is on syntax, continuity, and clarity. They also fact-check and sometimes save your bacon.

For traditional publishers, a copy editor can be someone who works in-house or freelance. They go over the manuscript with a fine-tooth comb (and yes, nitpick it), and then they return it to the editor, who reviews the copy editor's comments, weighs in (in the margins, formerly in colored pencil, now usually electronically), and sends the manuscript back to the author to consider all the copy editor's notes.

Copy editors do much more than monitor commas, but it's the commas that drive me nuts. I can spend half an hour staring at a comma that the copy editor wants to add (or subtract), trying to determine if I really want to add (or subtract) that comma. "What does it matter?" I ask myself after the first ten minutes, but there I am, ten minutes later, still agonizing over that little curve of ink.

It takes time to consider every note a copy editor makes. Even after so many revisions and so much attention to detail, it's a rare page that makes it past the Queen unscathed, and it doesn't take long for irritation to set in. This was especially true for the Sammy Keyes series, which seemed to have a different copy editor for each book, and every one of them threw the entire manuscript into past tense. They hated the way I switched tenses back and forth between past and present, since it did not adhere to standard grammatical style, and the pages came back to me completely bloodied with "corrections." It took many books for the copy chief to develop a guide that dubbed my style "California casual" and informed the copy editor that the switching of tenses was intentional, not author ignorance.

The flip side of that was my reluctance to recognize where improvement in the prose *was* needed. Early in my career I would have a knee-jerk rejection to the notes, telling myself that what I'd written made perfect sense and how could the Queen not understand what it meant?

But the fact was, she *didn't* understand. And if *she* didn't understand, maybe other readers wouldn't either. So, pages later and often grudgingly, I'd go back and revisit where the gap in understanding might have occurred. And usually, still grudgingly, I'd concede that there could be an element of confusion.

Which, over time, grew into the editorial version of "the customer is always right": The reader is always right. If the reader doesn't get it, it's probably not on the page. And being defensive or trying to explain what you meant is not going to lend clarity to what you've written. There's always another way to say it, and working to find it is part of your job as an author.

Now sometimes, despite their superior knowledge of syntax, you *are* right and they're just wrong. What's nice is if the editor has run block in this situation *before* you see the marked-up manuscript. If the editor disagrees with the copy editor's correction or note, she will line out the correction and write *stet* beside it. (*Stet* derives from Latin and means "let it stand," or, basically, "ignore this correction/comment/suggestion.")

When my editor's not sure about a correction, she'll write *Wendelin?* or just *W?* alongside the copy editor's note, and then it's up to me to decide if I'm going to take or stet the change.

It's always a relief to have made it through the dance with a Comma Queen. When it's over, you do a little curtsy, send back your revision to the editor, and bow out.

Phew.

And then, a couple of months later, you get called back onto the dance floor by a *different* Comma Queen.

That's right. After the corrections have been made to the final manuscript, it goes through the mill again; now it's set in type, emerging as a first set of page proofs. And instead of going back to the original copy editor, the page proofs are sent to a new person: a proofreader. This person's job is to make sure that the page proofs match your final manuscript exactly—but also to find any errors that the copy editor, or your editor, or you, the author, might have missed. New eyes. New approach. New commas to consider.

And here's the hair-pulling part:

A comma that the copy editor added—a comma that you might have agonized over for half an hour and finally agreed to—the proofreader may cut out.

Oh, for the love of Oxford commas.

I think adding one makes things clear, precise, and readable.

Others, however, find it to be superfluous, overused and fussy.

So you as the author are forced to choose, which sometimes

means taking a stance against the in-house style guide. (By the way, this whole process is usually performed one more time—when the first set of page proofs is marked up with corrections and a second set of page proofs is created and sent to a second proofreader. And if there are still more corrections, there could be still more corrected page proofs.) Eventually there comes a point where you are so completely sick of looking at your novel's pages that you don't even care anymore. Or, at least, that's the lie you tell yourself. Because after my book (meaning the page proofs) has, once again, been returned to my editor for final-final corrections and a few weeks have passed, I always panic. What if the corrections weren't done right? What if I missed something?

In that panic, I email my editor and beg, "Can I please, *please* give it one last look before it goes to press?" and promise her I'll turn it around in twenty-four hours.

And guess what?

I always, *always* find mistakes.

Sometimes substantial ones!

And I'm always, *always* glad for that last look through the page proofs before they become an actual book.

And then, finally, it *is* a real book. And guess what?

Someone finds a mistake in it.

Still, sneaky errors aside, when I was a new author, I had no idea what went into prepping a book for traditional publication or how much time and effort got devoted to making sure everything about the book was just right. I'm grateful to the Comma

Queens (and the King in-house at Knopf who has overseen the final page proofs for almost all of my books), because I know that without them, there would be a lot more errors caught by readers, and some of them (like the time I misspelled *Shakespeare*) would be downright embarrassing.

# 53

## BOOK COVERS AND ILLUSTRATIONS

I am not an artist. However, like most people, I have definite opinions about art. So it's hard to be left out of the design process of a book I've spent years writing and perfecting. But typically, authors—especially new ones working with larger publishers—are not consulted much if at all on art or design.

Obviously, I had a pretty rude awakening to this with *How I Survived Being a Girl.*

To the author, excluding the person who wrote the book is a bit of a head-scratcher. Who knows the book better than the author? And it's *their* book. Why can't they have the art *they* envision?

The answer is that we can't be masters of everything. Publishing houses have designers who (with input from the editor) either create the book jacket or work with an artist to create one. Their career focus has been on book art and design. It is their profession. And although art is in the eye of the beholder and we'd like to see our own book dressed in a way that's aesthetically pleasing to *us*, we may not be aware of what look will best serve our book in the current marketplace. It's the design team's job to create a cover that will entice the intended audience to pick it up, open it up, and sink into the magic of our words.

For your first book, you will likely get a preliminary rendering with a note saying something like *We hope you love it as much as we do!*

And that's sincere. They hope you do. And maybe the cover is better than you could have imagined . . . and maybe it's not. If it's not, take a step back, cool off, and understand that that hunchback may be a much better choice than you can know, given that your expertise is words, not art or the marketplace.

The most befuddling case of being-kept-out-of-the-art-loop is with picture books. If you're a writer-illustrator, that's obviously not an issue. But if your dream is to write a picture book and you don't have art skills, know that it's the design team at the publishing house that selects the illustrator. Do *not* submit illustrations done by your friend or neighbor or someone you know from your writers' group, even if you think they're perfect or brilliant. That is not how it's done. (There are lots of resources on how to format and submit picture-book manuscripts. If you want to join that field, study them!) Editors and art directors choose the illustrator, and you will likely have little say in who that is.

You will also not be allowed to talk to them.

That's right. It's your story, but they don't want you weighing in on the art. Sounds nuts, but let me de-befuddle it a little: We authors have a vision for the art. We have opinions. And we'd like to tell the illustrator what we see and think and want, all the way down to the freckles on our character's cute little face.

It's hard to be creative when someone's looking over your shoulder, breathing down your neck, rendering opinions. Shoot, it's hard to *breathe* when someone's doing that. How would you feel if you were at your computer, typing your story, your imagination frolicking along, and all of a sudden you realized someone was standing behind you, reading every word.

You would slap them back and say, *Go away! I can't write like this!*

So, there it is.

That's why.

They can no more create art knowing you're watching and wanting to guide them than you can write with someone looking over your shoulder.

Let them do their thing.

Once you've built a relationship with an editor and have demonstrated respect for the restrictions and decorum, they will start to let you in a little. For *The Running Dream,* my editor sent four potential covers and asked if I had a preference. I definitely did, and they went that route. That was a first in almost fifteen years of working together.

For the Sammy series, the original hardback covers—the

puzzle-piece design—were created by an illustrator and the publishing house's design team. The books were beginning to come out in paperback with the same artwork, but when *Hotel Thief* won the Edgar, a decision was made to change the paperback art to a more realistic look, while the hardback art continued in the puzzle-piece design.

About six books in, the paperback covers were changed again, this time with bright packaging and a focus on the humor of the books. The hardcovers continued in the puzzle-piece design, and the paperbacks were now more cartoony. And although I thought the art was fun and well done, I started to get feedback from teachers and booksellers that the covers weren't hitting their mark. The art appealed to boys in third and fourth grades, the name Sammy implied a boy protagonist, and middle school kids—especially girls—were not picking them up without being told what was inside the covers.

When the end of the series was on the horizon, it seemed like a good time to consider a new look, but repackaging an eighteen-book series is an expense that needs justification. And if you're going to do it, you want to do it right. So I embarked on a quest to gather information. I came up with a questionnaire that I sent to book people, solicited input via social media, listened to booksellers, and got feedback from thousands of kids during school visits.

After a good nine months of gathering data, I compiled all the information in an easy-to-process summary and sent it, along with some general art ideas (realistic middle school girl, skateboard, high-tops), to my editor. The steps between that and the approval for repackaging seemed to take forever, but in the end, repackaging *was* approved, and then began the process of deciding on the art.

Sammy Keyes books mix adventure with humor with mystery with coming-of-age with serious themes. How can you capture all of that in the cover design? What do you focus on? Should the art be realistic or stylized? Humorous or scary? Should it have a bright background to catch the eye? A dark background to convey a different vibe? Or maybe a white background to pop the art and have it fit in nicely with the look of many of my stand-alone books?

The evolution of the current covers did not happen overnight. What the experience taught me is that the choices are infinite, and that a seasoned art director is invaluable. It was fun to be involved, but even though I was the person who had written all eighteen books, even though I was the one who had gathered all the data, I did not have final say. Which, in the end, I was fine with, because they backed up their decision with marketing data. As long as we were in the ballpark of a style that addressed the data—whether it was data I'd supplied or from the publisher—I was just grateful to have my series get the boost of a new look.

One last note for those of you who want to be illustrators: Like authors, sometimes you have to go back to the drawing board. Be willing to do so. It's part of the process. Also, keep building your portfolio. Find your style, but keep an open mind. Being flexible, agreeable, and willing to revise will make art directors and editors much more open to working with you.

# 54

## BASIC FINANCE

While we were living in the Box House, our exit plan involved a piece of land a short drive north that had a view of the Pacific Ocean. It was an unimproved lot with difficult access and a steep footprint, but oh, the view. Part of the reason we continued to live in the Box House was that we were making payments on the land, but also because we were paying to engineer the foundation of a house we hoped to build on that land. It wasn't a fancy house—a basic two-story rectangle—but wow, the engineering that was needed to access the lot and secure the house to the bedrock. It became a big black hole sucking up our paychecks.

Fortunately, one of my former students mentioned that her father was a building contractor. He was an immigrant from Holland, so there was the Dutch connection, but he also had a deep respect for teachers and became committed to helping us get the house built.

With our savings completely spent down and now up to our eyebrows in loans, we finally moved out of the Box House and into our own at about the time that *Sammy Keyes and the Hotel Thief* won the Edgar. And uh-oh, the assumptions our new neighbors—and my old colleagues—made. You could see the wheels turning in their minds as they looked around, took in the view. Their reaction had nothing to do with *Dream big, work hard, don't give up.* After all those years of us working long shifts and weekends and teaching extra night classes, after all our juggling of schedules and chronic sleep deprivation, what people thought was *This is the house that Sammy Keyes built.*

Because everyone knows: Authors are rich.

There was a time when I thought that getting a book published would mean my family's financial troubles would be solved, so I was guilty of similar thinking. And since it's not polite to ask about money (and since most people like to promote an aura of financial success and don't mind the misconception), that assumption tends to be perpetuated. So instead of leaving you wondering (or perpetuating the myth), let me outline the financial basics of being an author.

*The advance:* This is the money a publisher will pay you up front—before the book is released for sale. This can range from nothing to a whole lot, with "a whole lot" being the exception rather than the rule. *Advance* is short for *advance against royalties,* which is a significant detail, explained shortly.

*Agency fee:* This is the percentage your agent will take from your advance, their slice of the pie for the services they provide.

Again, this figure varies, but it applies to your advance as well as to royalties.

*Taxes:* Any money you receive is taxable. To be safe, you should set aside about thirty-five percent of everything earned for Uncle Sam. Especially if you have other forms of income. You do not want to be caught off guard come tax day.

*Royalties:* Your contract will have details regarding the percentage you will be entitled to for the sale of all forms of your book. This can include hardcover, paperback, book club, audio . . . Whatever percentage is specified in your contract is the amount you get for the sale.

*Advance against royalties:* Whatever amount your publisher pays you up front must be recouped through your slice of the sale of your book (your royalty) before you see any additional money.

As a rule of thumb, after taxes and agency fees, you should count on getting about half of your advance. And you will be in no danger of spending that amount all at once, because you will not get it all at once. The likely payment scheme is that the publisher will pay one-third of the advance on signing, one-third on delivery of an acceptable manuscript (after you and the editor have gone back and forth a bunch), and one-third on publication . . . a schedule that can take a year and a half (or more) to complete.

And remember, it's an *advance against royalties.* What does that mean, exactly? Well, imagine a piggy bank where your publisher collects your contracted royalty percentage from the sale of every book. To keep the math simple, let's say that an author gets ten percent of the list price of their hardcover book. If that book sells for $20, the author gets $2 for each book sold. Ebooks have a varied pay structure, but paperbacks have a royalty rate that will plunk about $0.50 into the piggy bank.

Over time, the publisher collects these $2 and $0.50 royalties, *plink, plink, plink,* until the piggy bank holds the amount of the full advance. After it reaches the advance amount, the publisher will send any additional royalty amounts (the accumulation of extra $2 and $0.50 earnings from book sales) to you (via your agent), along with a royalty statement—something that happens only twice a year.

When you begin to earn royalties beyond the advance amount, your book has "earned out," and that is cause for celebration. The reality, though, is that a lot of books never earn out. The other reality is that if your book hasn't made good strides toward earning out during its first year, your publisher might not be willing to publish your next book.

Most authors dream of the big advance and are dying to win the race to the top. But it's hard to build a career if you have books that don't earn out, and there's a better chance of not earning out with large advances.

Generally, the advance amounts are modest. My advances for *How I Survived Being a Girl* and the first Sammys were on the low end. It took me many years to begin earning as a writer what I had made as a schoolteacher. And once I made the leap to full-time writer, I no longer had the health benefits, the 401(k), or any of the other perks that come from traditional employment. It was also hard to manage a budget with income coming in so sporadically (and unpredictably).

Some authors start out with a flash-bang advance, but if that's not you, don't be jealous. You may feel like you want it all *now*, but I truly believe it's better to build a career over time. I never got a flash-bang advance, but I have a large catalog of books—some of which have been going *plink, plink, plink* for over twenty years—because I have been a good financial investment for my publisher.

We used to have a rule that you couldn't come to our new house unless you'd been to the Box House. It was definitely still a rule when my editor came out to California for that first-meeting conference. She had built in an extra day to stay with us, so on our drive north I told her about the rule. And since we'd barely moved and I still had the Box House keys, I swung by the old place and let her in.

She blinked a lot but didn't say much. And on our walk back to the car, she said, "I'm glad I didn't know."

Because knowing would have complicated things.

Was she wanting to buy a book from me because it was really good and she was eager to work with me?

Or because she wanted to help me?

I'm glad she didn't know either. The joy of her offer would have been marred if our living situation had influenced it.

I'm sharing all this to illustrate that although we hear about the books that hit like lightning, the reality is that most authors never "strike it rich."

So what's your motive?

If you're in this for the money, a lottery ticket might serve you better.

If you're in this for the love of writing, please, keep writing. Hopefully you'll have a career that's slow and steady. It really is the best way to win this race.

*Plink, plink, plink.*

---

# 55

# TRADITIONAL PUBLISHING VS. SELF-PUBLISHING

Another common question from writers wanting to be published is *What about self-publishing?*

I get why they ask.

Boy, do I get it.

So let's compare and contrast and then you can decide what's best for you.

As you've seen from the previous chapters, a traditional publishing house invests considerable wo/manpower in taking your project from manuscript to press. To move the book through the developmental process, they pay you an advance, they pay an editor, a copy editor, proofreaders, and a design team, along with assistants and associates. They pay to print and warehouse physical copies of your book. Then they pay an in-house publicist, a marketing team, and a sales force to get your book noticed and stocked in bookstores and libraries around the country.

You get none of that with self-publishing. You can hire a freelance editor, but that's not cheap and the job they do does not involve investing their career or reputation in your work. They may love your story, they may hate it. As long as you pay them, they will work on it. It's a completely different arrangement than the one you'd have with an editor who pays *you* for your work.

I do know a lot of fiction writers who have self-published. They're excited about their creation, excited to press the Publish button, excited to have local book signings. But to a person, that excitement gives way to a common frustration: After the goodwill of their friends and family has been wrung out, their sales dry up. With all the effort they're making on social media, with the price point online so reasonably low, why is nobody buying their book?

The discouraging reality is that it's drowning in an ocean of books, and no single person's individual efforts are going to be able to keep it afloat. Maybe if you're famous to begin with or have some other means of getting your book noticed, you can join the exclusive club of people who have had big success self-publishing, but just pressing Publish is not going to get the results you dream of.

Writers looking to get published often think the traditional publisher's royalty pay structure is a rip-off. But when you consider all the costs involved in producing a book, and that publishers sell to bookstores at a price point much lower than the retail figure from which the royalty is calculated, you start to realize that their profit is not much greater than your royalty percent. And part of where that money goes is into getting your book noticed.

On the self-publishing side of things, you get to keep most of the money from sales. But keeping most of the money from next to no sales is not what you envisioned when you pressed Publish.

It's not what anyone wants.

So for fiction writers who want lots of people outside their sphere of family and friends to read their book, I would say that self-publishing usually leads to disappointment.

Not always, but usually.

*However,* self-publishing may be the way to go in certain cases.

If you have an area of expertise, if you have knowledge about a niche subject, or unique information about historical events, self-publishing a nonfiction book can make sense. Again, don't expect to sell a million copies, but if the subject is a passion of yours, there are likely people all over the globe who share your passion and might be interested in reading your book.

I've also seen schools effectively use self-publishing for collections of student essays, poems, or art. Sometimes these are done as fundraisers, but usually they're just a fun way to get students more fully engaged in a project.

Self-publishing also makes sense for what I consider the most valuable thing any person can write:

Their memoirs.

Or family history.

Maybe you want to fictionalize your story and try to place it as a novel, or maybe you just want to get it out so your kids and their kids and *their* kids will know and understand you. Passing down stories is a valuable, time-honored tradition. By documenting yours, you'll create family treasures, and by pressing Publish at a self-publishing site, you'll create a work that's easy to read, easy to share, easy to keep and pass down.

My cousin has done an amazing job of self-publishing. She is a cancer survivor whose daughters were young teens during her surgery and treatments, and her girls wrote a book about ways to be helpful to a parent who's going through such an ordeal. A niche subject, but one that people searching for books related to fighting cancer will stumble upon. The goal wasn't to make a lot of money, but to provide something that could be helpful to others.

Since then, my cousin has self-published her mother's artwork, her father's poems, her grandmother's journal, and other family memorabilia. It's a fascinating collection, and without self-publishing the contents would still be buried in boxes in the garage and, in another generation or two, would likely be buried at the dump.

So there's a case to be made for both traditional and self-publishing, depending on the situation, the book, and the author's desires. Ask yourself what you want. Maybe you want your book in stores and libraries around the country. Maybe all you really want is to hold your book in your hands. Or maybe you just want people to be able to download it for free. Every case is different, but if you define what you really want and you're armed with knowledge of the benefits and drawbacks of each publishing path, at least you can make a reasoned choice about how to proceed.

· VII ·

# FINAL THOUGHTS

## 56

---

# DODGING DEATH

When people close to you die, death suddenly casts a darker shadow. It moves from something over *there* to a real and very present fear inside your heart.

After my dad died, and later my brother, it felt like Death was lurking, ready to spring out and nab someone else I loved.

Or me, if it could.

So I ran. If I kept moving, if I kept busy, if I kept mentally occupied, I could push away that shadow and escape its creeping terror. But when I stopped, that shadow would sneak up on me and, if I let it linger in my mind, consume me with dread and despair.

Before I became a mom, I simply didn't *want* to die. After I became a mom, I had a rational reason, way better than simply not wanting to die: I had two innocent little lives to protect. My kids needed me!

As my kids got older, I held on to that reasoning. But I

developed a backup reason, which, as my children grew into their teen years and didn't rely on me as much, became less of a backup and more of a focus: I had to live long enough to get to the end of the Sammy Keyes series.

The deeper I got into the series, the closer I edged toward the final book, the more consumed I became with not dying before I got to the end. What if I cashed in my chips before Sammy's father was revealed? What if I was pushing up daisies before we got to the root of evil Heather's issues? What if I bit the dust before Sammy got her first kiss? What if I kicked the bucket before I pulled everything together?

My readers would kill me!

The last sentence of any book is important. I probably spend more time perfecting the final sentence than any other line in a novel. It's your swan dive off the page. You want your toes pointed, your arms spread majestically, your body perfectly aligned, and your head held high and proud.

The last sentence of a long series?

Wow. That's a leap off the high dive. And you can't just get to the end of the board, look down, and stumble off. You have to prepare! Then you have to run at it strong, take a powerful bounce, expose your heart, and soar.

I had known what the last sentence of the Sammy Keyes series would be for about five years before I got it down on paper. Nobody else knew because, well, if I let it out, it would spoil everything.

Everything!

Also, it felt like if I shared it or wrote it, my reason for why it was super important for me not to die would be gone. *Oh, that's how the series ends? Okay. Well, at least we aren't left hanging.*

Besides, sharing the last line would be like delivering the punch line when you haven't finished setting up the joke. It doesn't hold up, doesn't make sense, isn't funny.

Not that this last line was a punch line, or any laughing matter . . . but then again, it kind of was. It was a line that would resonate with people who'd held on through all the twists and turns of Sammy World. A random person picking up the last book to see the last line would go, *What's the big deal?*

But a Sammiac?

There would be tears.

So in this case I didn't agonize over the last sentence— I knew exactly what it was going to be.

I agonized over getting to it!

And it became my new excuse for why Death needed to stand back. I had to finish the series. I had to write that last sentence.

Sammiacs needed me!

So maybe it was because I'd held that last line inside for so long, or maybe because I'd projected such importance onto reaching it, but when the last sentence of the last Sammy Keyes book came out of my fingers and onto the screen, I lost it. First the tears streamed, then the gasping started, then my husband looked over from his desk and asked, "Are you all right?" and that's when the floodgates opened. He came over and held me as I bawled my eyes out. I'm talking great gulping gasping blubbering convulsing bawling. And when he understood what I was saying, when he saw the words on the screen, when he realized that after almost twenty years, the story was finally at its end, he held on and just let me let it out.

So, lucky me.

I lived long enough to finish Sammy's story.

I lived long enough to see my kids to adulthood.

I'm grateful and happy, and part of me is more than a little surprised.

Which should (and does) give me a certain degree of peace, but the truth is, I'm now looking around for new excuses. New reasons why Death shouldn't catch me yet.

Maybe I'm greedy.

Or just human.

Or maybe we all live best when we have something to live for.

# 57

# BE THE OXYGEN

Despite all the camping and wilderness survival experience I'd had in my life, there was one thing that the troubled teens in *Wild Bird* are required to do that I had never done.

Start a fire with friction.

I'd seen other backpackers attempt it, but never success-fully, and it just didn't seem worth the effort to pursue doing it. I was more into the architecture of the firewood. My signature structure had fine kindling in the center and a tepee of small branches over the kindling, overlaid with a larger tepee and encased by a log cabin that tapered slightly inward.

This design served me well in the one-match challenges we imposed on ourselves (and each other) as campers. From a young age, that was the goal—start the fire with a single match. Except for the quick rake of a phosphorus sulfide tip over rock, friction played no role in the lighting of fires. Even *my* parents would spring for matches.

But in wilderness therapy camps, starting a fire with friction is something campers have to master to cook their food. There's no faking your competency in this skill.

There's also no faking it when describing it on the page. If I was going to write about it, I wanted to involve all my senses—to really *feel* it so my firsthand knowledge would find its way into my character's experience. Once I realized I had to tackle it, I got down in the dirt with my sticks and some cordage and gave it a shot.

Let me start by complaining.

It's a lot harder than you may think!

There's a fireboard (a small, flat board with a notch) that receives a spindle (a stick whittled to look like a dull pencil), which has cordage (thick twine or a shoelace), which is anchored to the ends of a bow (a stick with a gentle arch) and twisted around the spindle. The whole assembly looks like a big pencil twisted through a crude violin bow nose-diving into a notched board, and pressure is applied by pushing down on the spindle with a palmed, smooth stone.

Just getting the pencil-thingy in the bow-thingy took, like, twenty tries.

And once I finally had the bow-pencil-thingy nose-dived into the fireboard, I anchored the fireboard with my boot, pushed down on the spindle with the palmed stone, and pulled.

The whole thing fell apart.

I went back at it, again and again, and when I finally had the hang of the mechanics of it, I pushed and pulled—like speedy sawing—to create friction between the spindle tip and the fireboard.

Long before I saw it, the first thing I noticed was smoke.

My nose told me it was there.

I got super excited because, you know, where there's smoke, there's fire!

The procedure for starting a fire with friction is that the friction you create between the fireboard and the spindle produces a little coal that builds up on a leaf positioned beneath the fireboard's notch. That little coal gets transferred into a nest of dry grasses located at the heart of your waiting fire structure.

My tried-and-true, one-match fire structure was good and ready. I had the nest of grasses inside a kindling tepee, inside a bigger tepee, surrounded by a log cabin. I was excited to be smelling the smoke, and when the smoke showed itself like a genie rising out of the wood, I giggled.

My husband, who was standing by with a fire extinguisher (because, well, he knows me and my projects), was snapping pictures with his phone.

Any second now, there'd be fire!

I pulled and pushed the bow fervently, the smoke genie kept rising, and when I was sure there was a coal waiting for me under the board, I tossed the bow and spindle aside, pulled out the leaf, and saw . . .

About a quarter teaspoon of soot.

No coal.

Nothing remotely red.

"You need to go longer," my husband with the phone and fire extinguisher suggested. "And faster."

So I reassembled everything and tried it again.

And again.

And *again*.

My arms were aching and I was breathless and sweating when I finally, *finally* produced a coal. With shaking hands I transferred the coal into the kindling nest and . . .

The coal went out.

*Argh.*

But I had to do this. So I reassembled everything and produced another coal. I tried transferring it again, and again the coal went out.

I pulled the nest out of the fire structure so I could more easily transfer the next coal. That worked much better, and when smoke began expanding inside the nest, my very weary arms were greatly relieved.

Until the coal just . . . died.

"You have to blow," my husband said. "It needs oxygen to burn."

Duh. Of course. That's how I always got fires going. But here I was so exhausted that I'd forgotten.

Back to the fireboard I went and sweated out another coal. And this time when I transferred it over to the nest, I blew.

I could see the heat of the coal spread to the tips of the dry grass. Little twinklings of red. Little sparks. And while I was blowing, my mind made a connection to *Wild Bird*, to my poor lost character Wren:

This was what she needed.

This was what *all* kids needed.

Shoot, this was what *everybody* needed!

We hold tiny sparks inside us, and to bring them to life—to really make them burn—they need oxygen. Without it, sparks just die.

I was so distracted by this thought, this connection, that I stopped blowing.

And just like that, the sparks went out.

*Argh.*

So I went back to the fireboard, got another coal, transferred it into the nest, and this time I blew and blew and blew. Smoke billowed, sparks twinkled, but where was the fire?

My husband leaned in and added his breath, and suddenly *whoosh!* There was fire burning!

In my hands!

"Aaaaah!" I cried, and tossed it wildly into the air.

We managed to shepherd the burning ball into the fire structure without incident, but I was, I admit, glad for the foresight of a fire extinguisher.

Afterward, I had so much I could use for my story, but more than that, I had my revelation.

Sparks need oxygen. Lots of it. And no matter what our hopes and dreams are, we need to surround ourselves with people willing to blow oxygen onto our sparks. In our pursuits— and this is not limited to just creative pursuits—there will be naysayers. People who will tell you you're not smart enough or pretty enough or talented enough or strong enough or young enough or old enough or *whatever* enough. Don't let people like that anywhere near your spark. All of us face failure and discouragement, but instead of giving up, we need to find people who are willing to be the oxygen, people who will help us fan our sparks into flames.

This doesn't go just one way.

We need to be the oxygen for each other.

It's my hope that this book has served to blow air on your spark, whatever it may be; that you'll come back to it and reread the passages that give you courage or strength or hope, and that you'll move forward toward your goals. The best days of my life have been the ones when I've had hope in my heart, and the best way I know to create that is by putting hope in the mail. Send that query. Build that website. Take that class. Write that book. Try out for that team. Apply to that school or job that seems out of reach.

And when you find people who are willing to support you or help you, remember them, *treasure* them. And when it's your turn, be the oxygen for them.

Blow.

And blow hard.

Wren's revelation at the end of *Wild Bird* is that the first step in moving forward is learning how to light a fire inside yourself.

So here's to your spark.

May you find ways to ignite it, and keep it burning long and hot and bright.

# ACKNOWLEDGMENTS

My creative sparks could very easily have fizzled out if not for the gusts of oxygen supplied by so many. For over twenty years, the three strong and consistent winds on my embers have been my husband, Mark Parsons; my editor, Nancy Siscoe; and my agent, Ginger Knowlton. How warm and bright my world is because of you!

There have also been countless librarians and teachers who have arranged for me to speak on their campuses and have used my books to kindle a love of reading in their students. Thank you for sharing your hearth—your classroom or library is a treasured space, one I'm honored to have been invited into and to have my work occupy.

And thank you to everyone who encouraged me to write this book—I do hope it encourages you to write yours . . . or pursue whatever your dream might be.

Inside my publishing house are people who have helped shape and promote my books for my entire career. Thank you to everyone at Knopf/Random House—both in-house and in the field—who has lent breath to the cause, especially those who have diligently tended the flames since the first Sammy Keyes book.

Thank you, too, to the booksellers who have shown an undying passion for connecting readers not just to any book, but to the right book for that person at that time. Some of you have been hand-selling my titles for more than twenty years. How can I ever thank you for that?

And, of course, thanks to my family and friends, especially those who have taken turns hauling wood to the fire pit when I was in danger of burning out. Your steadfast support has meant the world to me!

And finally, to my fans: Your letters, posts, and reviews have been like passing the flame of one candle to the next—small gestures, perhaps, but collectively they have lit up my world. You. Have. No. Idea.

So, to all who have helped build the ring, haul the wood, strike the match, stir the embers, or lend me oxygen, please know that, with an eternal flame of thanks, this one's for you.

# WENDELIN'S WORKS
## REFERENCED
## IN THIS BOOK

# THE SAMMY KEYES MYSTERIES

Winner of the Edgar Allan Poe Award

"This sleuth delights from start to finish.
Keep your binoculars trained on Sammy Keyes."
—*Publishers Weekly*

# WILD BIRD

"A strikingly raw and emotional story. The first-person narrative perfectly captures Wren's cynical yet vulnerable teen voice." —*School Library Journal*

# THE RUNNING DREAM

Winner of the Schneider Family Book Award

"Jessica's determination to regain her old life and her passion
for running will touch everyone who reads this story."
—*The Examiner*

# FLIPPED

A *School Library Journal*
Top 100 Children's Novel of All Time

"We flipped over this fantastic book, its gutsy girl Juli and its
wise, wonderful ending." —*Chicago Tribune*

# *RUNAWAY*

FROM THE AUTHOR OF *FLIPPED*

**Wendelin Van Draanen**

# RUNAWAY

"Holly's lively self lingers in the way the best characters do. *Runaway* is certainly one of the best young adult books of the year." —*The Sacramento Bee*

# THE SECRET LIFE OF LINCOLN JONES

Winner of the Josette Frank Award
from the Bank Street College of Education

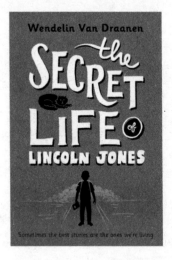

"A story with a perfect balance of mirth and poignancy."
—*School Library Journal*

# SWEAR TO HOWDY

★ "Van Draanen deftly hooks readers with her very first sentence and keeps their attention with a series of hilarious stunts right up to the shocking climax."
—*Booklist*, starred review

# THE GECKO & STICKY QUARTET

"A dastardly good read. Written with gleeful wit, rapid-fire pacing and snappy dialogue." —*Kirkus Reviews*

# THE SHREDDERMAN QUARTET

Winner of the Christopher Award

★ "Wa-hoo! for Shredderman, and kudos to Van Draanen for delivering a character-driven series that's spot-on for middle-graders and great for reluctant readers, especially boys."
—*Booklist*, starred review